ETHICS

NURSES AND PATIENTS

Edited by

Verena Tschudin BSc (Hons), RGN, RM,
Dip. Counselling

Illustrations by Richard Smith

Scutari Press · London

First published 1993

British Library Cataloguing in Publication Data
Nurses and Patients
  I. Tschudin, Verena
  174

  ISBN 1–871364–75–2

Contents

Contributors vii

Preface ix

1 **Confidentiality** 1
Verena Tschudin

2 **Informed Consent** 35
Richard Rowson

3 **Advocacy** 65
Diane Marks-Maran

4 **Responsibilities and Rights** 85
Verena Tschudin

5 **Accountability** 121
Diane Marks-Maran

Index 135

Contributors

Diane Marks-Maran   BSc, RGN, Dip N (Lond), RNT

Director of Academic Developments, Queen
Charlotte's College, Thames Valley University

Richard Rowson   BA (Hons) London

Principal Lecturer in Philosophy, University of
Glamorgan

*Diane Marks-Maran, Richard Rowson and Verena Tschudin
are all members of the National Centre for Nursing and Midwifery Ethics, London.*

Preface

Ethics is not only at the heart of nursing, it *is* the heart of nursing. Ethics is about what is right and good. Nursing and caring are synonymous, and the way in which care is carried out is ethically decisive. How a patient is addressed, cared for and treated must be right not only by ordinary standards of care, but also by ethical principles.

These ethical principles have not always been addressed clearly, but now patients, nurses, doctors and all types of health care personnel are questioning their care in the light of ethics. Their starting points and approaches are different, but their 'results' are remarkably similar. The individual person matters and the care given and received has to be human and humanising.

The way in which the contributors to this volume, and others in the series, address their subject is also individual and unique. Their brief was simply that what they wrote should be applicable to practising nurses. Each chapter reflects the personal style and approach of the writer. This is what gives this series its distinctive character and strength, and provides the reader with the opportunity to see different approaches working. It is hoped that this will encourage readers to think that their own way of understanding ethics and behaving ethically is also acceptable and worthwhile. Theories and principles are important, and so are their interpretation and application. That is a job for everybody, not just the experts: experts can point the way – as in this series of books – but all nurses need to be challenged and encouraged.

Emphasis is laid in all the chapters on the individual nurse and patient or client. Ethics 'happens' between and among people, and, by the authors bringing their own experience to bear on their chapters, they show how ethics works in relationships.

Great achievements often start with a small idea quite different from the end result, and so it is with this series of books. The initial proposal is almost unrecognisable in the final product. Many people contributed to the growth of the idea, many more were involved in implementing it, and I hope that even more will benefit from it.

My particular thanks go to Geoff Hunt, Director of the National Centre for Nursing and Midwifery Ethics, for his advice and help with this series.

Verena Tschudin

CHAPTER 1

Confidentiality

Verena Tschudin

Ethics is about people, and about what they do and say. It is concerned not only with doing the right thing, but also with how it is possible to foster right behaviour. Principles and codes of practice help, but eventually ethics happens mostly between two people, and in relationships.

Confidentiality has always been heavily emphasised in medical ethics. Nurses have had to think about it more closely, too, particularly with new approaches to and more holistic frameworks of nursing. This chapter looks at confidentiality in the light of principles and codes of practice and, in particular, in the light of the nurse's relationship with individual patients or clients.

This chapter, and others, not only answers questions, but also poses questions without answering them directly. These are the questions that address the readers' thoughts and personal values, on which their view of ethics is based.

The Patient's Rights

The Patient's Charter published in 1991 spells out the patient's right with regard to confidentiality:

> Every citizen has the following established National Health Service rights:
>
> . . . to have access to your health records, and to know that those working for the NHS are under a legal duty to keep their contents confidential.

 If confidentiality were so simple, there would be no problem. But as the UKCC Advisory Paper on *Confidentiality*

(1987) almost wearily points out, 'we live in a real world, and . . . sometimes there are a range of interests to consider'.

Although this chapter will consider the practitioner's point of view, confidentiality is the patient's *right*, and that side of the argument must be the starting point. What is confidential in health care?

In February 1992, the Royal College of Nursing (RCN) was in public conflict with St Thomas' Hospital, London, over an alleged breach of anonymity. The virology researchers at that hospital had issued a press release publishing the results of a detailed study of the blood of nearly 3000 women who attended antenatal clinics at the hospital. Of the approximately 490 women of African origin, 10 were reported to be HIV positive. 'Such detailed identification of a group of women at a specific hospital blows anonymity out of the water' claimed the

RCN (*Nursing Times* 1992). Statistics of all kinds are made available for many different reasons, but to what extent are they infringing confidentiality? How far can the results of medical and nursing audits be kept anonymous and yet be helpful where necessary?

While nurses and doctors are bound to confidentiality with regard to patients, this is not necessarily the case for other workers in health care settings. *The Bulletin of Medical Ethics* (1989) quotes an article written by a Canadian bioethicist who claims that, in a particular enquiry, the case notes of one patient were available to 'six attending physicians, 12 house officers, 20 nurses, six respiratory therapists, three nutritionists, two clinical pharmacologists, 15 students, four unit secretaries, four hospital financial officers, and four chart reviewers'. Over the life time of a patient and his or her notes in a hospital – or, in many cases, several hospitals — these figures could be multiplied several times, even without taking into account any notes held by GPs, community nurses, health visitors, etc. How confidential is such material?

The *Data Protection Act* 1984 protects computerised records, but typed or handwritten notes are not protected in the same way.

Wells (1988) writes of:

> an elderly gentleman with a tumour of the head and neck region which required major and disfiguring surgery. He had been married for over 60 years, was childless, and very devoted to his wife and she to him. On the day of the operation his wife was present in the hospital. She paced the corridors, smoked innumerable cigarettes and drank gallons of tea. Eventually the operation was over and she was persuaded to go to the staff dining room to eat. During her meal nurses at the next table were describing in vivid detail the procedures carried out on her husband. The enormity of her distress was terrible, but the reaction

of the staff, when faced with the situation was 'she should not have been in the staff dining room'.

This reaction is perhaps not unusual. Faced with a mistake, most people try to find someone else to blame. When it concerns someone else's rights, though, it is not a question of blame, but of responsibility. Nurses have a responsibility of confidentiality.

Confidentiality in the Codes of Conduct

The subject of confidentiality is specifically mentioned in all the Codes which bind nurses. To give just three examples:

- The International Council of Nurses (ICN) *Code for Nurses* (1973) states, 'The nurse must hold in confidence personal information and use judgement in sharing this information'.

- The American Nurses' Association (ANA) has a short *Code for Nurses* (1976) with lengthy 'interpretive statements' attached. Clause 2 of the code states, 'The nurse safeguards the client's right to privacy by judiciously protecting information of a confidential nature'.

- The United Kingdom Central Council (UKCC) has published its third edition of the *Code of Professional Conduct for the Nurse, Midwife and Health Visitor* in 1992. This states:

As a registered nurse, midwife or health visitor, you are personally accountable for your practice and, in the exercise of your professional accountability, must:

. . . protect all confidential information concerning patients and clients obtained in the course of professional practice and make disclosures only with consent, where required by the order of a court or where you can justify disclosure in the wider public interest.

The UKCC has produced a number of Advisory Papers to elaborate on certain aspects of the Code, including *Confidentiality*, published in 1987. This document defines some of the terms used in the Code, considers ownership and care of confidential information, and addresses the deliberate breach of confidentiality in the public interest or that of the individual patient or client.

The paper defines the four ways in which information about patients is disclosed:

a) with the consent of the patient/client;

b) without the consent of the patient/client when the disclosure is required by law or order of a court;

c) by accident;

d) without the consent of the patient/client when the disclosure is considered necessary in the public interest.

Category (a) is not a breach of confidentiality. Category (b) is somewhat more difficult. Moore (1988) says that the clause is 'legally accurate since nurses do not, in law, have a privileged relationship with patients as do lawyers with their clients; [and] the UKCC could hardly advise nurses to act in a way which might place them in contempt of court'. On the other hand, Clause 9 of the UKCC Code recognises the 'privileged relationship with patients and clients', which nurses should avoid abusing. The use of the same terms meaning different things in similar settings can be rather confusing.

Category (c) above is clearly one of care and respect, and also of 'etiquette'. The story related above (although not the nurses' conclusion) comes into this category. Nurses 'talk shop' just like other professionals, and sometimes this is for reasons of support and/or interest. However, in the dining room or on the way home on the bus may not be the best place.

The real difficulty arises with category (d). When do nurses know, and can they judge, when it is in the public's interest that confidentiality should be breached? The UKCC's Advisory Paper does not give clear guidelines other than to say that the nurse 'must have considered the matter sufficiently to justify that decision'.

There have been many cases in recent times in which health visitors and social workers have been accused of not caring enough for a particular child whom they could or should have seen to be at risk. Is a health visitor or community nurse to gain forceful entry into a home simply because she or he 'suspects' that a child in the home is at risk? Or search the house when she is told that the child is spending the night with a friend?

The advisory paper rightly quotes a health authority chairman who asks, 'Who is to define the public interest?' The paper lists serious crime, child abuse and drug trafficking as examples where confidentiality may be breached. But Moore (1988) asks, 'What is serious crime? Does the threat or admission of assault to another, revealed in confidence by a patient to a nurse, constitute more or less of a reason to disclose the confidence than evidence revealed in the same way of a multi-million pound City fraud?' Clearly, this is shifty ground. By looking at some specific examples, some of the issues that nurses need to take into account might become clearer.

Trust

The UKCC Advisory Paper *Confidentiality* (1987) believes that the focal word in the debate is TRUST (spelt with capital letters); 'To trust another person with private and personal information about yourself is a significant matter.' Information is passed from one person to another within a trusting relationship, and it is this relationship which has enabled the disclosure of the information (Marshfield 1992).

Taking the concept in its wide — not strictly legal — setting, it is clear that the 'privileged relationship' between practitioners and clients is of the utmost importance. Various new ways of nursing, such as primary nursing, key working, and partnership nursing, place increasing emphasis on this relationship. Perhaps before understanding confidentiality we should concentrate on communication and interpersonal relationship skills.

Any trusting and helping relationship is characterised by certain elements and attitudes on the part of the helper which are variously described as:

- non-judgemental;

- warm;

- genuine;

- empathic.

This basically means that the helper conveys that the client is unconditionally accepted as a person, for what she or he is, and is not judged on any arbitrary grounds or out of prejudice. If one person in the relationship is genuine and warm, then the other can potentially be so too. The humanity of each is acknowledged and confirmed, and this in itself is the basis for care, and physical and emotional health. Both parties have an interest in having and creating good relationships.

Trust seems to be the 'cement' which characterises the elements of relationships. Warmth, genuineness and empathy are all based on trusting: two people trust each other to be what they appear to be, say what they appear to be saying, and believe what they appear to be believing. There is a congruence between the behaviour and the attitude. Inevitably, this is easier said than done because relationships are fragile and vulnerable, but 'one of the qualities most of us admire in others and try to cultivate in ourselves is personal integrity. A person of integrity, in this sense, is one whose responses to various matters are not capricious or arbitrary, but principled' (Benjamin and Curtis 1986, p. 17). It is not only what people are, but also what they strive to be, that characterises them as ethical.

In professional relationships — as in personal ones — there are usually several interests to defend: 'The hospital nurse can be constrained in various and occasionally conflicting ways by the hospital (which employs her), the physician (with whom she works), the client (for whom she provides care), and the nursing profession (to which she belongs)' (Benjamin and Curtis 1986, p. 23). Nurses who are entrusted with confidential information have to consider their role in all these relationships, hence the difficulty of knowing which one has priority. In the case of confidentiality, however, there is the added burden of defining what is in the public interest.

Much of health care is based on utilitarian principles, that is 'the greatest good for the greatest number', but many health carers have been more influenced by deontological principles, that is, their personal duty as citizens rather than the outcome of any actions. Thus the 'accident and emergency department nursing staff who found that the unconscious patient they were treating had a gun on his person' (UKCC 1987) had to consider their personal duty: is it their responsibility to report this or is it only their responsibility to 'care' for the patient? They had also to consider the interest of the wider society: would people be harmed by this man if they did nothing about the information they had? But what of the patient's rights?

Confidentiality is a fundamental right. Whether the gun is real or the patient *says* he has a gun, the threat remains the same. How can one person's right to confidentiality be defended against another person's right to live in security, free from attack and fear of attack? Can nurses hold within themselves the claims of conflicting parties without having to take sides?

Ethical Principles

In order to make sense of ethical issues it is helpful to test them against certain principles. These have generally consisted of the five principles set out here, although their order may have varied in the literature.

Thiroux (1980) has outlined these principles in an accessible way, and in his book has demonstrated how they can be applied to medicine, business, education, and also specific issues such as capital punishment, euthanasia, abortion and problems of human sexuality. It is a versatile system, and worthy of consideration by any nurse. He divides the field of ethics into five principles: the principles of:

- the Value of life;

- Goodness or Rightness;

- Justice or Fairness;

- Truthtelling or Honesty;

- Individual freedom.

These five aspects cover most of people's relationships with each other.

The principle of the **Value of life** is, according to Thiroux, the first principle. It can be summed up in the simple phrase 'Human beings should revere life and accept death'.

This is his first principle because what all human beings have in common is life. The principle may extend to non–humans in certain societies. Clearly, the quality and quantity of life vary greatly between people and between societies, but people should revere life, and the injunction 'Do not kill' is one of the oldest and possibly clearest commandments that societies have upheld. Principles are, however, not absolutes, and this principle is infringed in abortion, euthanasia, suicide, war and capital punishment. The principle exists; it is up to society how it wants to interpret it by laws and moral standards.

One aspect of this principle is **respect for the person**. According to Campbell (1984), 'respect . . . implies a relationship of involvement with other persons, such that our choices and intentions are governed by their aims and aspirations as well as our own' (p. 94). The 'golden rule' states that we should treat people how we would like to be treated. Jantzen (1991) has given this a new twist by saying that we should not only treat people as we would like to be treated 'but how they would like to be treated'.

The principle of confidentiality can be seen within this context of treating others and treating ourselves. It is not simply 'I keep your confidentiality if you keep mine', but a question of respecting the other person as a person, a human being in his or her own right. What keeps societies together is the relationships which people form with one another and with causes, and these exist on the principle that there is intrinsic value in each life.

Valuing and respecting another person means valuing every aspect of their life, not just parts of it. It is not possible to say 'I value your right to health and wellbeing but I don't value the information you give me about it', implying that I judge how I deal with that information. However, none of this is absolute. It mut be clear that any right and any principle can and must be overridden by stronger moral considerations. In the case of confidentiality, this must be 'the public interest' or the greater good of society.

The principle of **Goodness or Rightness** is that which really defines ethics. Ethics is about being good and doing right, and what these are and mean, and codes and commandments try to shape human behaviour and human motivation. Put the other way, this principle tries to define what should not be done and how people should not be 'bad'. If everybody consistently acted rightly and with only the best intentions, there would be no problem. But life is not so easy. What is good for one person may not be good for another. Personal interests may conflict with societal interests, or the interests of one group may go against those of another. Nurses, too, as has been shown above, have to defend differing interests in any working day.

How does this principle affect confidentiality? In medical ethics the priciple of Goodness or Rightness has often been split into two:

- **beneficence**, or the principle of doing good;

- **non-maleficence**, or the principle of not doing harm.

Confidentiality is a person's right, and therefore keeping confidentiality is 'doing good'. By the same token, keeping a confidentiality could be doing others harm, and if this is the case, confidentiality should not be upheld. If innocent people are likely to be harmed, almost any principle can be overruled. The point then is, who are the 'innocent people'? Are they the ones who constitute the 'public interest'? Simply put, yes they are, and they includes any who might not be able to defend themselves physically or emotionally.

The 'goodness' of this principle also needs a little elaboration. What people consider to be 'good' will colour what they consider to be 'right'. Life, liberty and the pursuit of happiness have been declared as 'inalienable' by the Declaration of Independence of the United States, but other 'goods', such as knowledge, beauty, self-expression, peace and security, are also considered as generally valid. Out of these aspects have arisen, particularly since World War II, a series of human rights which are also intended to be in the public interest and to protect the innocent.

Confidentiality is part of the right conduct of a professional toward a client. Codes and declarations try, as far as possible, to direct behaviour by giving guidelines of professional conduct, and confidentiality is high on any nursing and medical list of important professional considerations.

In order to achieve certain 'goods', such as happiness, people are usually willing to undergo some pain or hardship. The term 'good' should therefore 'be defined in the context of human experience and human relationships rather than in the abstract sense only' (Thiroux 1980, p. 132). A doctor or nurse, therefore, in order to achieve personal and professional status and satisfaction (good), may have to be prepared to suffer some hardship. Since the professional relationship rests on trust, the building and keeping of that trust is vital.

The next principle, that of **Justice or Fairness**, follows very closely on that of good and right. Good and right do not only have to be done, but they have to be seen to be done, and this is evident in justice. A good person acts rightly, and this is perceived as justice. Actions are consistent, not arbitrary, and attitudes are congruous, not selective. Justice is the principle which is most evident in health care, particularly in situations such as the National Health Service. Everyone has the right 'to receive health care on the basis of clinical need, regardless of ability to

care; [and] to receive emergency medical care at any time'
(*Patient's Charter* 1991). However, the reality for patients
is often not so simple: some wait longer for operations
than others; some have access to a particular type of care
and others don't; one child may need a transplant but only
gets it after a plea in a national newspaper; those
with money can pay for private care and those without
spare cash simply have to await their turn — or so it
seems.

Various good reasons are given for any of these situations to exist, and in a climate of finite resources someone
suffers — not usually those who can shout loudest. But
is it even feasible that all services should be equally available to everyone? Some people may never need them.
One person's food may literally be another's poison. The
principle of justice demands not necessarily that everyone
has the right to every opportunity, but that 'everyone
must have an equal opportunity to acquire these things if
they desire them' (Thiroux 1980, p. 135).

The principle of justice demands that confidentiality be
applied equally to all patients and clients who come into
contact with health care professionals. A's information is
as confidential as B's, even if between A and B are all
the cultural, racial, class, colour, sex, religious and other
possible differences. These things should not influence a
worker: care should be given without judgement of the
person.

Justice is done between and among people; it is not
abstract, but a living experience. It is, therefore, precisely
in this living experience that confidentiality manifests
itself. Does a nurse make some information public to help,
protect and save others — the wider public, the many —
in the name of justice? Or does the nurse, equally in the
name of justice, protect one person because that nurse
cares about that one person and would like to continue to
be concerned about each individual and the individual's

personal rights? A nurse's own integrity, professional relationship, values and conscience alone can be the guide in these decisions.

The principle of **Truth–telling or Honesty** is as old as the hills — but not in medicine. The Hippocratic Oath makes no mention of truth, and neither the ICN Code nor the UKCC Code of Professional Conduct mention it, although the UKCC's Advisory Paper *Exercising Accountability* (1989) does consider truth in the light of informed consent.

Thiroux (1980, p. 135) thinks that 'this . . . may be the most difficult of all the principles to try to live with', and even the compiler of the Ten Commandments circumscribed it by saying, 'You shall not bear false witness against your neighbour' (Deuteronomy 5:20).

This principle, too, is lived in relationships, and because people are vulnerable in relationships and protect themselves, truth is often an early casualty. Despite a clear injunction, people frequently lie to one another, and lying and dishonesty may even be justified. Nevertheless, 'a strong *attempt* must be made to be truthful and honest in human relationships because morality, in the final analysis, depends on what people say and do' (Thiroux 1980, p. 135).

When this principle is applied to confidentiality, it is clear that anything kept confidential has to be kept as it was told, and anything which might have to be disclosed should be disclosed as it was told, not embroidered or only partially told. Indeed, in this case 'the truth, the whole truth and nothing but the truth' is perhaps the only guideline.

The last principle, that of **Individual freedom**, often also referred to as **autonomy**, is sometimes put as the first principle (see chapter 2). It is argued that human beings are free agents first of all, and that any morality stems out of that fact and realisation. Thiroux (1980, p. 128) puts it last because:

> people, being individuals with individual differences, must have the freedom to choose their own ways and means of being moral *within the framework of the first four basic principles* . . . individual moral freedom is limited by the other four principles: the necessity of preserving and protecting human life, the necessity of doing good and preventing and avoiding bad, the necessity of treating human beings justly in distributing goodness and badness, and finally, the necessity of telling the truth and being honest.

This principle has to do with equality of human beings themselves. Kant's Imperative, to treat everybody, including oneself, always as an end and never as a mere means, points to this principle, and principles of equal opportunities also point to individual freedom. People should be free to express themselves — so long as they also adhere to the other principles.

Individual freedom is the basis of democracy and also the free market. Both these 'goods' have their limitations, although they have proven to be more enduring than other social systems.

The principle of Individual freedom is perhaps the one which speaks most clearly about confidentiality. It must be the health worker's own individual privilege and decision to keep or divulge any information gained. In that very freedom, of course, lies the difficulty. Principles are not absolutes, and therefore no-one has absolute freedom to do anything; freedom is bounded by respect for life, doing right, being just and honest in all one's dealings. Someone cannot arbitrarily decide what to do with freedom, but has to weigh it up against the implications of the other principles.

In order to see all these principles in action, it is useful here to look at a story and relate the principles to it.

The five principles in action

- Mr A had been admitted for surgery for possible cancer of the bladder. The nurse had done the admission interview and he had told her he had married again only a few months ago. Two days after his operation she answered a telephone call from someone called Betty who asked if she would give Mr A her love. The nurse went to his bed and gave him this message. His wife was with him. She looked curious, and asked who Betty was. 'Oh, one of the managers at work', said Mr A, in a somewhat embarrassed way. The nurse thought no more about it. About 10 days later, the same thing happened again: a call from Betty; the nurse gave Mr A the message while his wife was with him. She said, 'Your managers seem very caring people'. He laughed rather awkwardly. Later in the day when his wife had left he asked the nurse over as she was passing, and beckoned her close to him. He simply said, 'That was my second wife. My present wife is the third, but she only knows of one other marriage'. The nurse was rather taken aback by this, as it had come so unexpectedly. She went to the office and was about to say 'Guess what . . .' when she checked herself. He had told her this in confidence. However, she thought, if Betty phones again, and the other staff answer, they would spare Mr A embarrassment if they knew not to give him the message while his wife was there. The nurse reasoned that Mr A was able, really, to deal with Betty himself, and that for the other staff to know of Mr A's other marriage would not contribute to any better care by them.

In this story, the principle of the value of life is applicable in several ways. Mr A was in hospital having his condition treated. The nurse had respected the information about his health and circumstances that were given, and had not judged him or his information. The nurse cared for him well, and gave him the telephone messages as they arrived, thus showing respect for the patient. His wife was with him, thus also showing that

family and carers are not to be excluded, but rather encouraged to take part in any care.

The principle of Goodness and Rightness overlaps with the first principle, as indeed they all do, and 'Ethics is a reflective examination of the moral life in search of self-knowledge and practical guidance' (Niebuhr 1963, p. 48). It is a question of being good and doing right, and how these are learnt, acknowledged and carried out. What does it mean in this case for the nurse to be a good person who does right? What does it mean that the environment of care is good and right?

Personal goodness on the part of nurses is shown by their care. They respect their patients and their relatives, and care for them. Nurses are people of integrity and practitioners of quality, and as such they adhere to their professional code of practice.

In doing this, they act rightly. They do right by other

people. Their actions allow others to be good and do right, and so fulfil their human potential. Doing right means caring for people and their surroundings. In this way, nurses are responsible for their environment, equipment and the atmosphere within which they work.

The nurse in the example above was concerned that she acted rightly after having been given Mr A's news. She was concerned about his health and his relationships with his wife. She was concerned not to cause embarrassment and so possibly destroy a relationship. She questioned her responsibility and decided that:

- she was not responsible *for* Mr A's relationships with people outside her ambit;

- she was responsible *to* Mr A and the information he gave her;

- she was also responsible to herself and her profession in the way she dealt with the issue of confidentiality.

H Richard Niebuhr, whose theory of Response Ethics will be examined shortly, seemed to suggest that 'morality is more a matter of relationships than of principles, of situations than of obligations, of dialogue than calculation' (Kliever 1977, p. 114). Thus the nurse in this story was right first to consider the relationship with her patient, and then to decide on that basis.

The principle of Justice and Fairness is perhaps more implied than obvious in the above story. It is possible to think that because the nurse acted in this way in this situation, she will do similarly in other situations, that is, other patients can rely on 'justice' (or equality) being a principle which applies in this environment. The nurse also considered that all nurses should have the same information as herself so that they could all act similarly. Justice demands that all can give the same care, and not that some can do better because they have more (or better) information. However, the principle of respect for the person overruled the principle of justice in this case, showing clearly that it must often be the case that one aspect has priority over another, even though they are, in theory, equal in importance. Morality, as pointed out above, depends more on particular relationships and individual situations than on obligations.

It is the principle of Truthtelling or Honesty which is most clearly affected in this story. By his dishonesty Mr A has created a situation which now causes difficulty for other people, possibly causes them to act unethically, and at least causes them to challenge their own values, obligations and responsibilities.

The situation described does not show that Mr A asked the nurse to help him to rectify his behaviour. The nurse might have challenged his behaviour, but she had no right to judge him in the sense of refusing to care for him once she had been given this information. This demonstrates quite clearly how important the right to confidentiality is for the patient, and how the carer must try to hold information in such a way that it does not damage the individual.

This leads to the principle of Individual freedom. The nurse had to use her powers of decision-making based on her ability to exercise free will. She did this by deciding that this information:

• was for her ears only;

• would not substantially help others in their care of Mr A.

But what if she had decided otherwise? She would have taken one of the four options described by the UKCC (1987) for breaching confidentiality:

• If she discussed with the patient that she should tell

the members of her team what he had just told her,
and he agreed, then there was no breach.

- If his present wife found out, perhaps by accident,
of another marriage and she sued Mr A for it, impli-
cating the nurse in any way by colluding with any
cover-up, then the nurse would have to tell in court
what she knew.

- If, as she almost did, the nurse went to the ward
office and said 'Guess what . . .' and only then
realised what she had done, she would certainly have
breached confidentiality by accident.

- If she considered that this was a serious crime —
which it cannot be described as unless other pertinent
information came to light — then she might have to
disclose information in breach of the principle. She
would have had to consider the public interest, or at
least the interest of other parties. The principle of
Individual freedom gives her that privilege and,
together with the principles of Value of life, Goodness, Justice and Truthtelling, she has to decide what
is her responsibility, what would lead to the best
good and least harm, and what would eventually
have the best outcome for all involved.

This short analysis of the story shows how, in any
decision, ethics as a whole is challenged. It is not just one
aspect which is either infringed or confirmed; ethics is
like dominoes: act ethically and all the pieces stand; act
unethically and, one after the other, they all fall.

But the question remains: how, or on what basis, does
a nurse decide to act in breach of confidentiality? It is
impossible to give guidelines such as 'in a prescribed cir-
cumstance act this way'. This would indeed be unethical.
Niebuhr's (1963) 'pattern of responsibility' in his

Response Ethics is, however, a useful guide to decision-making.

Niebuhr's Response Ethics

H Richard Niebuhr (1894–1962) was a political theologian who taught at Yale Unviersity for much of his working life. His influence has increased in recent years on both sides of the Atlantic. His theories on Response Ethics are contained in a slim work entitled *The Responsible Self* (1963).

Niebuhr points out that Deontology (Duty Ethics) asks 'What is the law?', 'What ought I to do?' In this we recognise the *citizen*. Teleology (and Utilitarianism) asks 'What is the goal?', and thus we recognise the *maker*. Response ethics asks 'What is happening?' and demands a response. Thus we recognise the *answerer*, and Niebuhr's logic of: response — response-*a*bility — respons*i*bility. The three stances of maker, citizen and answerer are not exclusive of each other, but rather complement each other, particularly in today's climate of synthesis as opposed to the rigid adherence to one system or theory.

Response Ethics is based on a 'pattern of responsibility' which in turn emphasises the meaning of responsibility. There is a distinction between responsibility *to* and responsibility *for*: 'To be responsible is to be able and required to give account *to* someone *for* something' (Niebuhr 1946). This happens within social relationships. To be responsible means being a fully functioning person in relation to other persons.

The pattern of responsibility which Niebuhr outlines is as follows: a challenge presents itself, eg information is given to the person. This causes a *response* in the person in the sense of feelings being activated, heart rate rising, fear being experienced, etc. This is essentially a bodily response, but it then translates into an *interpretation*, ie

memories and anticipations come into focus, eg 'Last time
something like this happened, the consequence was . . .'
or 'If I do this now, what will happen is . . .'. The challenge is interpreted in the light of feelings *and* experiences.
The action chosen is not arbitrary, but is taken with
accountability, that is with a sense of responsibility for the
past and the future. If this accountability is ethically correct, the outcome is one of *social solidarity*, meaning that
something greater has happened than was present before
the challenge. If the interpretation and therefore the
accountability are not ethical, but egoistical, then there is
social disintegration. In other words, the person has a
choice, and this is the moral action which is a 'social and
affective responsiveness' (Kliever 1977, p. 121). Niebuhr
insists that it is not a theory which makes people decide
one way or the other, but the 'heart', that is, the whole
person, particularly the feeling side of a person: the side
which is in touch with relationships.

Niebuhr sees his pattern of responsibility represented by
the two main questions 'What is happening?' and 'What is
the fitting answer?'

Response Interpretation	} What is happening?
Accountability Social solidarity	} What is the fitting answer?

An adaptation of this outline is:

Response	What is happening?
Interpretation	What would happen if . . . ?
Accountability	What is the fitting answer?
Social Solidarity	What has happened?

To make some sense of this pattern, and to be able to use it in decision-making, it needs to be elaborated somewhat.

Let us start with the *challenge*. This is usually something unexpected and surprising. Because of this, it makes an impact. Most people prefer to live their lives quietly, not being unduly upset, and therefore when a challenge presents itself they are not prepared for it and find it difficult to respond to it. Those who present the challenge do not necessarily do it to upset, but have perhaps thought about something for a while and then cannot hold back any longer. Two such situations are:

- A patient in hospital is undergoing chemotherapy. As the nurse fixes the drip, they talk together about children, and the patient says, 'You know, I sexually abused my niece for a long time when she was a child'.

- A community nurse is visiting a young woman with moderate diabetic problems. On checking the patient's insulin stock the nurse discovers a quantity of powder in a container and casually asks what it is. The patient admits that it is crack.

Nurses have long wondered how they can prepare themselves for the question 'Will I die?' asked out of the blue. To be told about sexual abuse out of the blue is not so very different.

Being ill or in hospital is a moment of truth for many people, and although they may not be in imminent danger of death, they want to 'sort things out', or feel the need to confess their past misdemeanours to someone. A caring nurse is often the most appropriate confidant in such a situation. The 'challenge' which is presented to a nurse is therefore often unexpected and overwhelming, and definitely demands a response.

The *response* may instinctively be one of 'fight or flight', or one of being so shocked as not to be able to move, but it is a response which is experienced first of all in and with the body. This is the most distinctive aspect of Niebuhr's

Response Ethics. The other theories of ethics do not consider feelings to be so important and so all-pervasive. This
is perhaps also why his ethic is particularly applicable in
health care. The patient's or client's side is also taken into
account here, in the challenges that nurses and doctors
often present to their clients by way of diagnoses, results
of tests, proposed treatments, etc. The patient also experiences a response, and can possibly no more cope with it
than can a nurse who has been told something shocking
by a client. The 'fitting answer' which is eventually given
is thus seen to be happening within a relationship. Indeed,
the answer, if it is fitting, is ideally given within a relationship of mutual understanding, knowing in the 'heart' what
is involved for the other. The relationship is based on
being human together — or co-humanity, as Niebuhr
calls it — and thus on empathy.

The question 'What is happening?' is therefore most
pertinent here. What is happening to the nurse who wres-
tles with this challenge? What is happening to the client
that he wanted to give this information? What is happening between these two people, now privy to some information which has changed their relationship? The analysis
of what is happening should encompass as much as possible of the situation, the lead-up to it and anything which
is pertinent. By considering what is happening in the body
and in the surroundings, a kind of assessment is made of
the situation which may help to throw light on anything
relevant. What is happening to the nurses in the two
situations above? Do they feel fear at having been told
and now having to cope with that knowledge? Do they
censure the patient for having done this act, or for being
a drug-user, gambling with health and life and probably
not cooperating with treatment regimes? It is not so much
a question of 'Why does it happen?' but simply of being
aware of what is happening so that the situation can be

assessed through the awareness which this question fosters.

The next phase in the pattern of responsibility is *interpretation*. Once the basic assessment has been made, one then starts to interpret. Like chess players, people remember what has happened in the past in similar situations and speculate on what may happen in the future. Niebuhr is unique among ethicists in spelling this out so clearly. His concern for people, and his insistence that decisions are made within relationships, led him to see that this is a vital step. Most other ethical theories jump from the challenge to the decision by simply seeing only the personal duty, or the greater good to be achieved via a theory, but do not much consider how people 'tick'. And people do not normally decide along theoretical lines, but from the 'heart', from what seemed right at the moment, or following a hunch. Having considered any feelings associated with past experience, the next step is always 'What would happen if . . . ?': if this course were taken, A would follow, or that course, then B. This is the question underlying any planning, and may have to be asked several times over. It is an experimental question, and a fundamental one for any experiment (Schön 1991, p. 145). If the nurse told someone of the patient's sexual abuse, what would happen? How should it be told? To whom? What would be the consequences for the nurse? For the patient? For any others involved? What would happen if nothing was told to anyone? Did the patient tell the nurse this information so that it would be passed on and something be done about it? This aspect of ethics has to be taken very seriously, and is vital for a good decision. Too often people do not believe that they can ask such questions, and that they do have the choice. Because decisions of practical care have often to be made immediately, nurses believe that it is the same for ethical decisions, but this is not so. The more that questions of interpretation can be considered in all their possible forms, the better.

The term *accountability* as used by Niebuhr may be somewhat misleading. He is not considering account-ability in terms of management and facts as it is usually understood today, but in terms of relationships. Responsi-bility requires of people that they account for their responses, that is, that having once decided, they stay with their actions and follow the consequences through. What guides most people in their ethical actions is a need to look for patterns and meaning in life and relationships. Thus Niebuhr is clear that it is not the right or correct answer, or the one which is most easily achievable, which is demanded, but the *fitting* one. It is not only the one which is most suitable in a given situation, but the one which, after considering all the given circumstances, is most fitting for the people involved and their relation-ships. Being accountable means showing a kind of dependability in actions which stems out of experience and clearly points forward with consistency. An ethical decision is then 'made as part of a total conversation that leads forward and is to have meaning as a whole' (Niebuhr 1963, p. 64).

The nurses in the two scenarios above have to give a fitting answer. The information given by one patient, and allowed to be discovered by the other is too serious to be dismissed. In the one case another — innocent — human being has been made to suffer, and the other situation involves breaking the law. The nurse — as a responsible citizen and professional — cannot stand by or turn away disinterestedly. The information has to be disclosed.

According to the UKCC (1987) there are four possible ways of disclosing information:

- With the consent of the patient. In these cases, this is the most ethical stance to take. The two parties may have to work together to the pattern of responsibility just outlined, and look at all that is happening and might happen. They may have to look at length at the various options and possibilities of disclosure, of how, when, where, to whom and what (ie what else may have to be disclosed).

- Without the consent of the patient or client when the disclosure is required by law or order of a court. This situation does not seem to apply in these cases.

- By accident. If the nurses in the two scenarios act ethically, they might consider discussing their possibilties with a colleague. This might be overheard, or used wrongfully by that colleague. It must be kept in mind that despite every effort made to keep something confidential, accidents do still happen, and plans not to disclose certain information can go wrong. Any information which is confidential should therefore be guarded particularly carefully.

- Without the consent of the patient or client when the disclosure is considered necessary in the public interest. These two cases probably do not warrant precipitate action, but the situation described in the Advisory Paper *Confidentiality* (1987, p. 4), where Accident and Emergency staff found a gun on an unconscious patient, will need action before the patient has had time to recover consciousness.

Whatever the 'fitting' answer turns out to be, it is the one which is also the most accountable. The people concerned have to make the decision, implement it and be able to stand by it.

The nurses in both scenarios had another option in addition to the four mentioned above. They could have helped their patients to disclose the information themselves to the police. This might be a far more taxing way of setting about righting a wrong, but it may also be the most creative one for all concerned, and the police would normally consider such action in the defendant's favour. This course of action would require skill on the part of the nurses, and enormous self-awareness and courage on the part of the patients.

Niebuhr's Response Ethics is based on the premise of relationships, of co-humanity and of a *community's* moral life. Any answer which enhances these aspects must be the fitting one. Anything, therefore, which empowers a person and enhances personal potential is fitting in this context.

The fact that Niebuhr sees *social solidarity* as the outcome of this process is not surprising. It is not simply the consequence of an action which matters (as in Teleology) or the action itself (as in Deontology), but the consequence of any action has to be for the greater good of all involved (as in Utilitarianism) and of society as a whole. Such a community (be this a family, a working team or a nation) is then bound together, because of the action, in a common cause and reciprocal loyalty. All members are affected by an action (or challenge), all strive to interpret it and find the fitting response. This gives the community a pattern and meaning in its life together which was no doubt there all the time, but is now strengthened.

The two nurses in the scenarios should think about this. In their planning (What happens if . . . ?) they should envisage what the outcome (What has happened?) might be, and they should strive for the most harmonious outcome possible, that which unites the community most.

It is evident that that is not something which happens overnight. In human relationships one has to take both a short-term and a long-term view. People and situations can change in ways which could not be envisaged, for both better and worse. However, with the quite radical belief in the potential and goodness of human beings which Niebuhr advocates, there must be hope that good will prevail. That good may, however, have to be coaxed, gently challenged and responded to with every bit of warmth, genuineness and empathy possible.

Social solidarity ends with the quality of wider relationships being enhanced, thus going back to the initial response which asked the two main people involved to examine their positions and responses. However, their response*a*bility has now become a respons*i*bility. If the initial response was a creative one, the outcome will now be one of greater wholeness and creativity.

It is not easy to envisage such greater outcomes when faced with an initial problem which perhaps seemed shocking at the time. The point made earlier, that there is very often time to consider a problem first, is worth keeping in mind. By seeing all the 'What ifs?' it may be that the creative possibility can emerge — and it is worth waiting for that.

The pattern of responsibility can be viewed as being cyclical or, perhaps better, as a spiral. Not only does it go round in circles, but each time the circle is widened.

It is not surprising, perhaps, that this also corresponds to the familiar pattern of the Nursing Process. Like that, the pattern is not just a theory, but also a model for a decision-making process in ethics. By having given three scenarios in this chapter, it is hoped that it can be seen to work.

This still leaves two aspects of confidentiality to consider: what the public interest is, and whom to tell if disclosing information is necessary.

What is the Public Interest?

This question has been asked a few times already in the course of this chapter. Despite that, there is no easy answer to it. Having considered Niebuhr's Response Ethics, it may be possible to elicit some guidelines.

The last point of the pattern of responsibility is social solidarity. The outcome of any ethical act has to be the enhancement of people everywhere. This is a more holistic view than considering simply the greatest number of people possible or an anonymous public. It is also reached by responsibility and accountability, thus involving those people concerned in personal and creative ways. It is not simply a response of duty or of keeping strictly to laws and policies.

When information has to be disclosed, or confidentiality breached, as in the cases under discussion, it may be possible to consider the *community* involved: the wide circle of people who all contribute to its life. It may not be possible to do this completely in practice, but ethics is concerned with ideals to strive for as much as with giving fitting answers. When considering the 'public', it may at least be possible to see them not as an inert and remote entity, but as a community of people with potential.

To whom should Information be disclosed?

The answer to this question lies in the situation itself. No two cases are the same, so no two answers can be the same. Perhaps the only guidance which can be given here is that any information should be given only to the appropriate person or agency. If it is a question of a criminal act, the police should know, but if not, a social worker or doctor might perhaps be better placed to help. The UKCC Code of Conduct stipulates that nurses should always consider their patients' and clients' wellbeing first of all, and in the interest of social solidarity this comprises any helping and caring possible. It is not up to nurses to pass judgement. The person or agency who can help best should therefore have the information. Anyone else may not have the same interest, and may gossip, which is never helpful.

UKCC Advice

The Advisory Paper *Confidentiality* (1987) gives guidance on the deliberate breach of confidentiality, and, most importantly, says that 'responsibility cannot be delegated' (p. 11). However, when practitioners have to make a decision, they *'should always take the opportunity to discuss the matter fully with other practitioners* (not only or necessarily fellow nurses, midwives and health visitors), and if appropriate consult with a professional organisation before making a decision'. Thus the UKCC invites nurses to consult them, which is indeed what many nurses have found helpful.

The document goes on to say that 'once having made a decision the practitioner should write down the reasons either in the appropriate record or in a special note that can be kept on file'. Once the decision is made to publicise information, that decision has also to be defended.

It could be argued that it may be helpful to make notes right from the moment of first considering any action. Noting down any discussions and telephone conversations, and any personal reasons for acting in a particular way, may not only be helpful in any court or enquiry, but may also help in a personal decision-making process.

Niebuhr too, wrestled deeply with the problem of having to make choices 'between life's values and valuers', or preserving this group against that. His advice, as may be expected, is not categorical, but directly person-oriented: 'serve that value which is in greatest need of your service rather than what is rightly considered highest. [And] serve not only the neediest but also the nearest at hand' (Kliever 1977, p. 140).

References

ANA (1976) *Code for Nurses with Interpretive Statements*. Kansas City, MO, American Nurses' Association.

Benjamin, M. and Curtis, J. (1986) *Ethics in Nursing* (2nd edn.). New York, Oxford University Press.

Bulletin of Medical Ethics (1989) Patient access to records. **54**: 5.

Campbell, A.V. (1984) *Moral Dilemmas in Medicine* (3rd edn.). Edinburgh, Churchill Livingstone.

ICN (1973) *Code for Nurses*. Geneva, ICN.

Jantzen, G.M. (1991) *Connection or Competition: Identity and Personhood in Feminist Ethics*. Paper delivered at Society for the Study of Christian Ethics, Oxford.

Kliever, L.D. (1977) *H. Richard Niebuhr*. Peabody, MA, Hendrickson Publishers.

Marshfield, G. (1992) *Confidentiality Within Nursing Settings*. Unpublished paper.

Moore, D. (1988) Confidentiality: all sewn up? *Senior Nurse*, **8**(6): 6–7.

Niebuhr, H.R. (1946) The responsibility of the Church for society. In Kliever, C.D. (1977) *H. Richard Niebuhr*, Peabody, MA, Hendrickson Publishers.

Niebuhr, H.R. (1963) *The Responsible Self*. New York, Harper and Row.

Nursing Times (1992) RCN fury over anonymity breach. **88** (7): 8.

The Patient's Charter (1991) London, HMSO.

Schön, D.A. (1991) *The Reflective Practitioner*. Aldershot, Hants, Avebury.

Thiroux, J.P. (1980) *Ethics, Theory and Practice* (2nd edn.). Encino, CA, Glencoe Publishing Co.

UKCC (1992) *Code of Professional Conduct* (3rd edn.). London, UKCC.

UKCC (1987) *Confidentiality*. Advisory Paper. London, UKCC.

UKCC (1989) *Exercising Accountability*. London, UKCC.

Wells, R. (1988) Ethics, informed consent and confidentiality. In Tschudin, V. (ed.), *Nursing the Patient with Cancer*, Hemel Hempstead, Prentice Hall.

Further Reading

Johnstone, M-J. (1989) *Bio-Ethics, a Nursing Perspective.* Sydney, W.B. Saunders.

This is a very comprehensive text on ethics. The section on confidentiality is dealt with under the heading of Patients' Rights.

Tschudin, V. (1992) *Ethics in Nursing, the Caring Relationship* (2nd edn.), Oxford, Butterworth Heinemann.

This basic text highlights many issues in nursing and specifically deals with confidentiality. It also outlines Niebuhr's Response Ethics.

A video explaining confidentiality laws and how they relate to health care has been produced by Tunbridge Wells Health Authority. *In Confidence* also deals with rights under the Access to Health Records Act 1990. Contact Anne Tanner, Education Centre, Pembury Hospital, Pembury, Tunbridge Wells, Kent TN2 4QJ.

CHAPTER 2

Informed Consent

Richard Rowson

Giving consent to treatments and procedures is more than signing a document. It is also more than simply having the correct information to do so.

Informed consent is based on an understanding of individual autonomy, and also on the best interest of all concerned. How much can and should a patient know about a treatment? What are the limits to informing? These issues are dealt with in this chapter in a way which demonstrates that informed consent is one of the cornerstones of health care.

Introduction

'Informed consent' is the process of giving patients information about their illness and its likely development and treatment, so that they can give or withhold their consent to a particular course of action.

Many people consider that such consent should have high priority in health care, for both legal and moral reasons: Legally, once patients have consented to treatment, health care professionals have a defence against prosecution for assault; and Morally, because to treat people only after they have given their consent respects both their wishes and their right of self-determination.

These reasons seem so powerful that you might at first think that everyone must accept the case for seeking informed consent and respecting patients' wishes whenever possible, but not everyone does accept this. Many people think that it is inappropriate on many occasions,

and see a danger in giving too much importance to patients' wishes. One doctor was heard to remark, 'If the patient's wishes are supreme, that is the end of medicine.'

How can such very different attitudes exist among people engaged in the same sort of work? It is the purpose of this chapter to help you understand the moral arguments by which these different perspectives are reached, and then to consider the extent to which you think informed consent should be part of daily nursing practice.

The Moral Background to Informed Consent

The value of individual autonomy

There are two main views which dominate the thinking about morality and give rise to many dilemmas in health care.

The first view is that respect for individual self-determination is of supreme moral importance. This has been held by many traditions, religious and secular, down the ages, and is a conviction many people hold. One of the most influential secular explanations as to why self-determination is so important was given by Immanuel Kant (1785), an 18th century German philosopher. He claimed that individuals must be free to make up their own minds about what is right and wrong if they are to be morally responsible for what they do.

If we do not allow people this freedom, we treat them like cogs in a machine rather than persons. Cogs simply react, turning one way or another solely because of the pressure of other cogs, but 'persons' have the potential to decide for themselves how to act. They can appraise their situation, work out the options, weigh up the reasons for and against different courses of action and decide what to do. They can form plans, purposes and intentions, and aspire to live in accordance with principles, ideals and values to which they have committed themselves.

In this view, it is morally essential to show 'respect for persons' by ensuring that people are able to make as many informed decisions and be as self-determining as possible. If we do not show respect, we fail to acknowledge their dignity and worth as persons, denying them responsibility for the way they live their lives.

Respect for persons is frequently referred to as respect for 'autonomy', which comes from the ancient Greek word for 'self-rule'.

Respect for autonomy in society

Respect for individual autonomy is a value widely acknowledged in modern society. It is enshrined, for instance, in Article 18 of the United Nations Declaration of Human Rights, which states: 'Everyone has the right to freedom of thought, conscience and religion'.

The moral value we put on autonomy and self-determination is fundamental to the view that democracies have a better system of government than totalitarian regimes. Democracies offer their citizens at least a token of political self-determination by allowing them to vote occasionally to indicate their choice of government, while totalitarian regimes do not give their citizens freedom to express their political views — treating them more like cogs. One of the main concerns of human rights movements, feminist movements and organisations fighting for the interests of minorities — such as the elderly and disabled — is that everyone has a right to have their views heard and respected (see chapter 4).

Respect for autonomy in health care

Respect for autonomy is acknowledged, too, in many aspects of health care. Nurses are no longer regarded as the doctors' handmaidens, whose duty is simply to obey orders, but as professionals capable of independent judgement and with a role to play in decision-making. Similarly, great emphasis is laid on the moral and legal importance of respecting patients' wishes and rights. As Bridgit Dimond points out in her book *Legal Aspects of Nursing* (1990, p. 85), in British law 'any adult, mentally competent person has the right . . . to consent to any touching of his/her person. If he/she is touched without consent or other lawful justification, then the person has the right . . . to sue for trespass to the person'.

There are reasons, other than legal and moral ones, which support the case for patients having an active role in decision-making. For example, some psychologists claim that people are more prone to depression the more helpless they feel. So patients who have no say in their own management, and see themselves as having no powers of decision-making, are more likely to feel depressed and lacking in self-esteem than those who are involved in making decisions. Depression can reduce the effectiveness of the immune system, impairing patients' ability to resist infection. In contrast, involving patients in decision-making can increase their motivation to get well and encourages them to believe that they can positively affect their own health. So, the argument goes, involvement in making decisions may be a way of improving patients' health (Weinman, 1987).

Respect for autonomy and the professional–patient relationship

If you accept the importance of patient autonomy, you will see the professional–patient relationship as one in which both participants have an active part to play, not as one in which the professional is an active expert with all responsibility for what happens, and the patient a passive recipient of what has been decided.

There are different views, however, on the degree of importance which should be given to patients' wishes. If they are given supreme importance and valued above all other considerations, then the patients' wishes become the deciding factor in all decisions on treatment, and the professional's expertise has a subservient role. In this situation nurses and doctors must inform patients of their condition and all possible options. If asked by patients whether they have a preferred option, they may state it, but must be careful not to bias their information in favour of it. They must then do whatever the patient decides. So, for example, if a patient demands a skin graft as a 'quick-fix' for an ulcer, the surgeon has to carry it out, even though the nurse thinks the condition would be better dealt with more slowly with dressings, without the risks and expense of surgery.

Many people object to this type of situation, pointing out that professionals as well as patients have autonomy, and in this case, that of the professionals is ignored. If you consider it is morally important to respect autonomy, can you accept a relationship in which the professionals' autonomy, to say nothing of their expertise and personal feelings, is ignored? Shouldn't respect be shown to them, too?

These issues have led to discussions about whether a process of joint negotiation might be needed. They point to the ideal model of the professional–patient relationship as a partnership, in which the professionals' knowledge is combined with the patients' perceptions of their needs, wants, estimate of quality of life, values, etc., as a basis for making the decisions. So, for example, if a patient refuses to accept strong pain-killers because she wants her mind to be clear, and the nurse knows that the patient does not realise how severe the pain will be, the nurse might explain the likely effects to the patient and hope to negotiate her agreement to accept a weaker dosage or use other means of pain control.

The moral value you give to respecting individual autonomy will obviously influence your view on the importance of seeking informed consent, but before we consider that, let us turn to the other major moral view.

The Utilitarian view

Many people think that, whatever we do, we have a moral obligation to try and make our actions produce the best possible consequences. Several religious and secular traditions stress this obligation, and many people think that it should be our sole moral concern.

Jeremy Bentham (1789), for example, a British philo-

sopher, took this view, and subsequent thinkers have
developed his approach, which is known as Utilitarianism
because it claims that the moral value of actions consists
in their 'utility' or 'usefulness' in bringing about valuable
results. From the Utilitarians' point of view, actions are
not intrinsically good or bad. They are only valuable as
means to an end. So, for example, being truthful and
honest are not valuable in themselves, but only if they
are likely to lead to states of affairs which we think are
valuable.

Our moral obligation, according to this view, is to act
in the way we think is likely to maximise benefits and
minimise harm. So, whenever we choose what to do, we
should consider all courses of action open to us, assess the
likely benefits and harms of each on everyone who may
be affected, and then choose the course of action we think
will bring the greatest benefits to all.

In his book *Moral Thinking* (1981), Richard Hare puts
forward the view that when we are assessing the likely
effects of different actions, we have a moral responsibility
to imagine how these effects will be viewed by other
people. We should try to put ourselves in their position.
From what we know of their likes, dislikes, cultural and
religious values and emotional situations, we should try
to understand how they would feel about the effects our
different actions might have on them. Then we should
strive not simply to bring about what we ourselves regard
as desirable effects, but to produce consequences which
suit the preferences of as many people as possible, including ourselves. Hare's view is that we benefit people by
enhancing their opportunity to live in ways they prefer,
and our moral obligation is to help them do this.

So, when working out what is in the best interests of
your patients, you should try to imagine how they would
feel about being affected in different ways. For instance,
you may think that an elderly patient in a terminal state

might prefer to be kept comfortable for her remaining life, rather than be subjected to painful invasive treatment designed to prolong her life by a few weeks or months. If so, this should be central to your assessment as to what is in her interests.

In this way Utilitarians try to take into account the wishes and perspectives of all individuals who may be affected by their actions, and, as patients are likely to be affected more than anyone else, priority should be given to their views and values.

Utilitarianism in society

Many people regard the Utilitarian approach as the right way to make decisions, whether in public or private life. For example, many major government decisions — such as where a new airport or road should be sited — are made only after a public hearing in which the benefits and harms of alternative locations are assessed.

Utilitarianism in health care

Health economists frequently take a Utilitarian view when they recommend that decisions about the allocation of health care resources should be made only after analysis of the likely costs and benefits of alternative ways of using them.

They often assess benefits in terms of QALYs — 'quality-adjusted life years', and suggest that a principal concern of decision-makers should be to produce as many QALYs as possible for patients (see chapter 1, Vol II). The idea of QALYs has been developed as a means of measuring the amount of benefit produced by different health care procedures (Cohen and Henderson 1988). A QALY is a unit of benefit, consisting of a year of a person's life, and the value of the year is decided by assessing the person's quality of life. 'Quality of life' is usually seen as the number of functions a person can perform, and at what level. So, the more able people are to perform well all the functions necessary to look after themselves — like washing, dressing, cooking, shopping, etc. — the better their quality of life is judged to be. One Utilitarian view is that we should give priority to health care procedures which produce the greatest number of QALYs (life years of good quality) for the amount of resources they consume.

Whether or not you agree with this particular Utilitarian view, the chances are that on many occasions you weigh up the likely effects of your actions before deciding what to do. After all, isn't one of the attractions of entering nursing the possibility of bringing benefits to humankind by promoting health and relieving suffering? People see this as a morally fine motive, and the health care professions enjoy the public's moral approval and respect as long as this is regarded as their main objective.

Thus many of the accepted duties and responsibilities of the health services are based on the conviction that health care professionals are right to deploy their knowledge, experience and skills to bring as much benefit as they can to their patients. Similarly, to learn how to do this is seen by many people as the main objective of much nursing and medical education. So we see nurses as having both a moral obligation and a professional responsibility to judge how to allocate their time and care between patients in ways they think will benefit them the most. Many people consider that nurses and doctors would be failing in their responsibilities if, having made these judgements, they then allowed them to be overruled by patients' wishes — especially if they were certain that acting in accordance with these wishes would not be in the patients' best interests.

How much attention do you think should be given to the patient's wishes in the following situations?

- A nurse is on a ward where one patient demands a lot of attention, but does not need any specific care, and another patient is in fact very uncomfortable and needs constant turning, but 'does not like to bother her'. Should the nurse give the amount of attention the first patient demands, even if the nurse knows it will result in the second patient being in greater pain?

- A patient constantly requests an expensive treatment, which has had much publicity as a new wonder cure but which the doctor is certain will not improve his condition and may well have severe side effects. Should the doctor conform to the patient's request? Shouldn't it be considered that providing this expensive treatment may eat into a budget which could be spent in other ways to bring greater benefit to patients as a whole? Since the doctor's budget, like the nurse's time, is a finite resource, shouldn't they both deploy their resources in the way they judge is likely to benefit their patients most?

When we consider questions like these we can appreciate some of the moral, professional and practical considerations behind the remark of the doctor that if patients' wishes are supreme, the end of medicine is in sight.

Utilitarianism and the professional–patient relationship

From the Utilitarian perspective, the right kind of patient–professional relationship is one in which the professionals use their expertise to decide what is in the best interests of the patients. The patients role is to comply, as the beneficiaries of the professional judgements. This is sometimes known as a relationship of 'justified paternalism' (Beauchamp and Childress 1989), though a better term might be 'justified parentalism'.

The relationship between autonomy and Utilitarianism in health care

Respect for autonomy and Utilitarianism, then, are two moral views which lie behind many judgements to act rightly. As we have seen, the moral demands of these views frequently conflict in day-to-day circumstances, and disagreements arise because of the different importance people give to each. Some think that respect for autonomy should always take precedence, while others think that the need to work for the best interests of all should do so. There are also those who think we should weigh their demands against each other, according to what we think is appropriate in each situation.

Let us now consider in more detail some issues of informed consent.

Seeking Informed Consent

How much should we tell patients about proposed treatment?

There are considerable variations in the procedures which people regard as 'obtaining informed consent'.

The practice of asking patients to sign a consent form, recording their agreement to be treated or to be examined, *before* they have been informed of their condition and the nature of the examination or treatment is clearly inadequate. 'Informed consent' has not been obtained since no informing has taken place.

Nor is it adequate to tell patients of their condition and the course of action proposed, but not give them any details of likely success rates, risks or side effects. Even if these details are given, but in a way which suggests that the patients are not expected to have any views on the matter, let alone ask any questions, then, again, this is not a case of 'informed consent', since patients have not been made aware that they really do have a choice of whether or not to consent.

For patients to give informed consent, we must at least tell them about their condition and the proposed care, examination or treatment in sufficient detail for them to understand its purpose and likely consequences, as well as the likely risks and side effects. This information must be conveyed in such a way that they realise that they can decide for themselves whether or not to accept that care or treatment, and whether or not to continue with it once it has begun. Only then can we claim that they have been informed sufficiently to make an intelligent and free decision on whether or not to consent.

As it happens, these minimal moral requirements for consent are similar to those required by English law, in which it is 'a basic principle . . . that an adult, mentally competent person has the right to refuse treatment and take his own discharge contrary to medical advice' (Dimond 1990, p. 89).

 Generally, doctors have a legal duty 'to take reasonable care that a patient receives appropriate information before any consent form is signed and treatment proceeds; the nurse should, as far as possible, take appropriate steps to inform the doctor if she discovers that this duty has not been carried out (Dimond 1990, p. 88). So, legally, doctors may leave the process of informing patients to nurses or others, provided they have taken 'reasonable care' to ensure that this is done.

 In order to be legally adequate, information must include as much detail of risks as would be 'accepted as proper by a responsible body of medical opinion (Dimond 1990, p. 92). Details of risks need not be given, however, if 'non-disclosure of risk of damage' (p. 92) would be accepted by such a 'responsible body'. Information about a risk should be given if 'a reasonable person in the patient's position would be likely to attach significance to the risk' (Dimond 1990, p. 92). However, a doctor may withhold information 'if on a reasonable assessment of his patient's condition he takes the view that a warning would be detrimental to his patient's health' (p. 92). This is a good example of legal opinion trying to balance the competing demands of respect for autonomy and the search for best consequences.

There is, then, a legal duty to inform patients of any substantial side effects of a proposed treatment, but we are entitled to withhold information if we think it is in a patient's interests not to know — an entitlement known as 'therapeutic privilege'. However, 'a doctor cannot withhold information about risks because he believes the patient would refuse consent if he was aware of them' (Dimond 1990, p. 94).

These legal principles apply to nurses as well as doctors, and the law seems to adopt the moral view that we should respect the autonomy of the patient up to the point at which it is against the patient's interest to do so. We should then be guided by Utilitarian considerations which ultimately take precedence over respect for autonomy.

Consider the following situations, then decide whether information given to patients should be restricted if we think it is in their interests not to know. Or do you think patients should be told everything?

- A childless couple in early middle age are seeking fertility treatment. Investigation shows that it has a very good chance of success, but there also emerges clear genetic evidence that the husband is highly likely to become demented in fifteen years or so. Should the couple be told of this possibility before they undergo the fertility treatment?

- An elderly woman is due to have exploratory surgery. Depending on what is found, the surgeon will be faced with various options, each with varying risks, outcomes and prognoses. Her condition may be terminal; on the other hand it may be only a relatively minor problem which can be easily overcome. The woman is frightened. The doctors and nurses think she would be worried by the complexities of what could be involved, and would in any case find them difficult to understand. Should she be informed of all the possibilities before the exploratory operation or not?

● When people are asked for their consent to HIV testing they are normally counselled to prepare them for the possibility of being found positive. But anyone who admits to having had such a test, even if the result is negative, is likely to have great difficulties with insurance companies. Is it the responsibility of health care professionals to inform patients of probable social consequences of treatment, as well as medical and personal consequences?

In considering these situations you may have felt torn between, on the one hand, wanting to enhance patients' autonomy by making them as well informed as possible and, on the other, not causing them what in your view is unnecessary anxiety. But how do you decide whether anxiety is unnecessary or not?

In the case of the childless couple, for example, you may have thought that, to be properly informed, they should know of the likely mental state of the husband in years to come before they decide whether or not to bring a child into the world. On the other hand, knowledge of his probable illness might well blight their lives through the time when they would otherwise be enjoying their child. A consideration against keeping quiet, however, is that some psychological evidence suggests that people generally cope better with difficulties the more they have been forewarned. So it could be in their interest to know, since they might still go ahead and have the pleasure of a child, cherishing the time more because it might not be long, then cope better than they might otherwise have done with the illness, should it come.

This example shows that, whenever we assess what is

in a patient's best interests with a view to limiting the information we give them, we have to rely on our knowledge of the particular case. There are no general rules which can make the judgement for us. Moreover, whenever we assess patients' interests, the best we can do is to reach a judgement about probabilities. There are no certainties.

Should we tell patients about alternative treatments?

The 1991 National Health Service's *Patient's Charter* says that patients have the right to be told of alternative treatments, not just one. And the NHS 1990 publication *A Guide to Consent for Examination or Treatment* says (p. 2) that 'patients are entitled to receive . . . information about the proposed treatment, the possible alternatives and any substantial risks'.

Many people consider that, however detailed the information we give patients about any proposed treatment or care, they cannot make a properly informed decision if they do not also know about other treatments which may be suitable; someone who thinks the only options are to accept or reject one form of treatment, when in fact there are other options, is seriously misinformed.

Against this, others have claimed that 'informed consent' simply implies informing patients sufficiently for them to give or withhold consent to one treatment, not giving them the right to demand from a range of possible treatments. They consider that, however much trouble we take to inform patients properly, it is sometimes impossible to convey the insights gained from the experience of working in health care. Consequently some patients, who have a poor grasp of the issues, believe their own judgements are as well-founded as those of the doctor or nurse. Moreover, as a result of the policy of informed consent, some patients confuse their right to

make decisions with their ability to do so. So, if we offer them the opportunity to choose from a range of treatments, rather than just accepting or rejecting one, we enlarge the scope for them to make poorly-considered judgements.

Do you think that patients should be given information about alternative treatments and care? Consider the following situation:

- A young man suffering from acute anxiety, stress and depression is referred to the local clinical psychology department. The psychologist he sees offers drug therapy, warns him about possible side effects of drowsiness, and asks him whether he consents to treatment. He accepts the treatment. Another young man with similar symptoms is referred to the same department, but sees a different psychologist, who suggests a regime of meditation together with regular counselling, and explains the likely effects. The patient accepts this regime. Later, when the two cases are

discussed, the psychologists agree that the patients had
similar conditions and that the different treatments they
offered are recognised alternatives. They say they proposed
different treatments, but did not offer the alternative,
because they subscribe to different — and opposing —
traditions in clinical psychology.

Since in this case neither patient knew of the possibility
of being treated differently from the way his psychologist
proposed, do you think their consent to what they were
offered was informed? Do you think they should have
been told about the alternatives? If so, do you think they
were entitled to demand the treatment their psychologist
did not favour?

If you think that patients should be told about alternatives, do you think it would ever be right to select the
options they are told about? Consider the following cases.

- A British man suffers from a rare and serious condition for
  which the best treatment has been pioneered by a doctor
  in Vladivostock. This treatment is not available to foreigners
  except at enormous cost. The patient might just be able to
  afford the treatment if he sold everything he possessed, or
  if his family and friends were able to persuade a newspaper
  to raise a fund. Should he be told of this possibility? Or if we
  think it would be less distressing for him not to know of this
  remote possibility, are we entitled not to tell him about it?

- A nurse knows of a treatment which may temporarily alleviate
  a patient's painful condition but, in her experience, the likely
  long–term side effects would far outweigh the immediate
  benefits to the patient. Should she include this among the
  treatments she tells the patient about?

Again we are faced with balancing respecting patients'
autonomy with judging what is in their interests. Many
professionals in fact consider it morally acceptable to
give selected information, if they think it is in the best
interests of the patient to do so. This accords with the

legally-permissible 'therapeutic privilege' mentioned on
page 47.

Some people think that, as well as restricting information in the interst of the individual patient, we should
sometimes restrict it to ensure the best use of resources
for all our patients.

Consider the following:

- A nurse on a very busy ward knows of several ways of
  managing the condition of a patient. She is certain that one
  of these will suit the particular patient far better than the
  others. Should she take the time to explain them all,
  indicating the likely effects of each, and ask the patient to
  choose?

- A doctor knows of an available treatment which is more
  expensive than others. In his opinion the extra benefit the
  patient would obtain from it does not justify the extra time
  and money the treatment would require. He honestly thinks
  these extra resources would bring more benefit to all his
  patients if used differently, so he decides not to mention it
  to the patient. Should he have done so?

  Compare this situation with that of a nurse on a ward who
  does not offer to spend extra time managing a patient in a
  way she knows would bring extra comfort, because she
  thinks she could bring more benefit to all the patients on
  the ward if she spent her time in other ways. Do you think
  she is wrong?

- A nurse has a friend who was helped to overcome
  agoraphobia by a course of hypnotherapy at a centre for
  complementary medicine. She has a patient with similar
  symptoms. She does not know much about hypnotherapy.
  Should she mention it to the patient, who will otherwise
  undergo drug treatment, which does not have a high
  success rate?

At this point it is interesting to look again at the NHS
A Guide to Consent for Examination or Treatment. It says
that patients 'are entitled to receive . . . information about

. . . the possible alternatives'. This could imply that information about the *full range* of possible alternatives should be given. However, on page 4, under 'Advising the patient', it says, 'Where a choice of treatments might reasonably be offered. . .'. This suggests that professionals may decide whether they think it is 'reasonable' to offer a choice *at all*, and, if so, they may *select* what they offer from the range of possibilities.

This quotation continues: 'Where a choice of treatments might reasonably be offered, the health professional may always advise the patient of his/her recommendations together with reasons for selecting a particular course of action'. Later (p. 9) it says, 'Consent to treatment must be given freely and without coercion'. There is clearly a fine line between, on the one hand, professionals giving their reasons for what they recommend and, on the other hand, coercing a patient to choose in a particular way, for it can be difficult to give your reasons for one particular form of treatment and, at the same time, avoid giving biased information. Yet presenting biased information undermines the moral value of informed consent, for patients are then not properly informed, nor is their autonomy respected, since they are being manipulated to choose in a particular way.

One way of trying to deal with this is, at first, to give information about alternatives and their risks and benefits as objectively as possible, without any comment as to which you recommend. Only then, in response to the patient's request for advice, do you give your reasons for your recommendation. In practice, however, it may be difficult to keep these two functions separate.

The upshot of these considerations then, is that, on the one hand, as health care professionals, we have a moral obligation to give patients as much unbiased information as we can, so that they can make decisions which are as informed and autonomous as they are capable of. On the

other hand, we may also have a moral obligation to select
and restrict information if we think it is in the best
interests of the individual patient, or of all our patients,
to do so.

There may, however, be another morally justifiable
ground for restricting information, as we shall see in the
next section.

How can we inform patients effectively?

If you accept that you have a moral obligation to inform
patients as truthfully as possible, you must also see it as
part of your obligation to communicate as effectively as
you can.

Your task is to convey your specialist knowledge to
patients, and to their relatives or friends, if the patients
wish to involve them. To do this you need to explain at
the right level, and in vocabulary they are familiar with.
In his book, *An Outline of Psychology as Applied to Medicine*,
John Weinman (1987, p. 164) gives many examples of
patients failing to understand terms nurses use every day.
One person, for example, 'thought "lumbar puncture"
was an operation to drain the lungs, and another took
"incubation period" to refer to the length of time a child
was to be kept in bed'. And a mother 'did not realise her
child was to be operated on when the doctor said he would
have "to explore".' You should consider the amount of
detail patients and clients can absorb. A welter of facts
can overwhelm them and prevent them from grasping
the points which are most relevant to them giving or
withholding their consent. There can be times when you
are morally justified in restricting the amount of information for this reason. On the other hand, of course, too
few facts can leave patients ignorant of important issues.
Since different people can cope with different levels of
vocabulary and complexities of information, you have to

judge what to say and how to say it on your knowledge of the individual patient.

If it is possible, use more than one occasion for the informing process; patients can be given an initial explanation of their situation, and be told that they can take time to consider what was said and think about questions to ask next time. This also gives them a chance to ask a friend or relative to come to the next discussion. The issues they are asked to think about will be completely unfamiliar for most patients, and they may need time to come to terms with them. Moreover, during a first session they may be under considerable stress and find it difficult to take in what they are told. In fact some psychological research suggests that 'around half the information which has been presented cannot be recalled within five minutes of leaving the surgery' (Weinman 1987, p. 166). A second chance to talk through the issues will help to overcome this problem. In addition, the patients' responses, after they have had time to reflect, can help you to judge the level and detail of explanation they can cope with.

It may even be better if patients can be given something in writing which they can take away to read. They can then absorb the information at their own speed, and discuss it with others. Some health authorities now have notes for patients about common conditions and the treatments available for them. Considering how most of us like to have the opportunity to read about a range of products before we choose which one to buy, it is quite surprising that we do not, as a matter of course, accept the need for written information about something as important as our health. Printed notes can also help to overcome the difficulty of giving unbiased information, when individual staff have firm views on what should be done.

Whether explanations are in speech or writing, short, simple sentences, free of jargon, are best. There is a fine line between making patients feel patronised and showing them that they are not expected to know much about the technical issues, so they should not feel ashamed of 'showing their ignorance'. Research suggests that 'typically patients . . . say that they do not want to look stupid by admitting ignorance, or that they do not want to cause trouble by asking for things to be explained' (Weinman 1987, p. 164).

It is easier for patients and clients and their friends or relatives, to be helped if they are as relaxed as possible. They can then concentrate on what is being discussed and feel free to interrupt, ask questions and express their feelings. The best way of doing this is to ask open questions, such as 'How do you feel about. . ?', and to let silences fall, so that patients realise they can take the initiative, and that there is time to listen.

Training in interpersonal skills is becoming accepted as a valuable part of nurse education, since effective communication is a vital part of caring (Tschudin 1991). Many people think it is appropriate for nurses to play an increasingly active part in informing patients, as nurses generally spend more time with patients than doctors do, so are in a better position to know the patients' characters. They can relate to them informally and discuss these issues as an integral part of caring.

Limits to informing

However skilled a communicator you become, there will be times when you are limited in what you can communicate. For example, however simply and carefully you make your explanations, some patients will never be capable of understanding enough of the relevant factors to make an informed decision.

It may also be almost impossible to convey to certain patients the likely effect of some treatments simply because the effect is hard to imagine, however well you describe it. This is particularly true of psychological effects. For example, one person involved in counselling couples about fertility treatments which lead to the birth of more than one child finds it extremely difficult to convey the often traumatic effects of multiple births. This may be partly because the couple's concern to have children makes them unreceptive to any counter-suggestion, and also partly because it is difficult for people who have no children to imagine the effects on their lives and relationships of not just one, but two or more babies. Such a situation raises the question of how much respect we should give to the wishes of patients who, we are certain, cannot imagine the effects of the treatment they request.

Since these limits of informing patients are sometimes inevitable, you should not see it as a sign of incompetence on your part if you come up against them.

Should we always try to obtain informed consent from competent patients?

Consent to treatment may be given in various ways: by signing a form, verbal agreement or gesture — such as rolling up a sleeve as the nurse approaches with a syringe. Though these actions signify consent, they do not necessarily indicate *informed* consent. They may be reactions or feelings of the moment, rather than decisions based on awareness and appraisal of relevant factors. Should we always attempt to obtain decisions based on this sort of appraisal from patients whom we judge to be capable of them?

Most people consider that we should not bring pressure on patients to go through the process of being informed and of making decisions against their will. If patients indicate that they do not want to discuss their condition and treatment, it is possible to ascertain first whether they genuinely do not want to think about the issues, or whether they are under pressure from relatives, friends or other professionals not to express their views. If it is clear that it is the patient's own wish to leave the decision-making to the professionals, the matter should be left to rest, since deliberately choosing *not* to make a decision is in itself a decision to be respected. By accepting the decision the patient's autonomy is respected and you are free to act in the way you think is in the patient's best interests. At this point, through discussion with colleagues and the patient's family or friends, a decision can be reached on the patient's behalf.

How can we decide whether someone is competent to give informed consent?

The capacity to make an informed decision about consent requires several types of mental ability: the ability to understand facts about the medical condition; to grasp causal connections between alternative treatments and their effects; to comprehend the probability of these effects and their long-term consequences; to think logically; to imagine situations and feelings; and to relate all these to the making of a decision.

It is a capacity, therefore, of some sophistication, and most of us who consider that we have 'normal' mental abilities may be acutely aware that our ability to think in this way can vary enormously. When you are tired, stressed, or unfamiliar with the issues of a complex problem, your ability to decide diminishes. You may, for example, be good at thinking through complex issues when deciding how to prioritise the demands on your time in a ward, but not so good at thinking through the less complex, but less familiar, issues of deciding which job to apply for.

If you can work out the level of complexity a patient can deal with, you can then respect the decisions made up to that level, but not feel obliged to accept those above it. For instance, you may decide that you should respect the wishes of a child of seven about what food he wants, but not his views about which alternative or long-term treatments he should undergo.

Similarly, you may judge that an elderly, mentally-impaired person may be quite capable of making judgements about how to spend the next hour, but not about whether she should have residential care or live at home. Although she can relate her immediate feelings to a decision about what she should do next, she cannot carry out the more complex judgement of how her disabilities would prevent her looking after herself in the future. To do this she would have to think logically and also imagine the consequences of different courses of action.

Since deciding whether a patient is capable of giving informed consent at a particular level of complexity is a difficult task, the more a case can be discussed with colleagues and others who know the patient, the better. Then any conclusion reached will be based on a wide range of experiences and views of the patient. Moreover, if a consensus view can be reached, it will avoid the danger of bias by any indvidual.

Another danger to avoid is the assumption that patients who are sometimes confused are never competent. Some professionals take the view that they are entitled to ignore patients' wishes, unless they have proof of their competence. Others consider that this is the wrong approach, and that we should assume that patients are competent, unless we can prove that they are not.

What should we do if we decide that patients are not competent to give informed consent?

If we consider that patients are clearly not competent, our moral obligation may, at first sight, seem welcomingly simple: since they are incapable of making autonomous decisions, all we have to do is decide what is in their interest and set out to achieve it.

However, if patients have been competent in the past, or are likely to be in the future, we may think we have an obligation to work out what they might wish us to do were they competent.

Let us consider first those patients who have been competent, and are likely to become so again. Perhaps they are unconscious, but are expected to recover. In these situations, if there is time, there is an obligation to discuss with family and friends how they think the patient would have chosen to be treated. Provided that to act in accordance with these supposed views would not harm the patient's chances of a recovery, the patient should be managed in accordance with these views. If this policy is adopted, there is a good chance that, on recovery, the patient will find the choice of treatment acceptable, and will feel that his or her autonomy has been respected.

Now consider the situation of patients who have been competent and are not expected to recover competency, but who have made a 'living will' or 'advance directive'. This is a statement made by a person who is competent as to how he or she wishes to be treated in the event of becoming unable to express his or her wishes. Since the legal force of such a document is uncertain, the legal and moral implications of carrying it out should be discussed with family, friends and colleagues. If possible, any decision to ignore or follow a living will should be made as a joint decision, since the decision can then take into account the knowledge of the patient and the moral perspectives of several people, and may be more defensible legally.

In the case of patients who have been competent, but have left no living will and will not recover, or patients who have never been competent, there are no elements of autonomy to consider. In such cases it is possible, in discussion with the patient's family, friends and colleagues, to ascertain what is in the patient's best interests by identifying any sources of pleasure or pain the patient has experienced in the past, and to consider how suffering can be reduced and possible sources of pleasure provided for.

In the case of children who are judged to be not yet competent, but who are expected to be so one day, it might again be possible to make decisions about their best interests in consultation with their families and with colleagues. But here 'best interests' should not simply be thought of in terms of pleasure and pain, but in terms of giving the children as many opportunities as possible to develop their potential. In this way their chances of becoming self-determining, confident adults in the future may be enhanced.

What if things go wrong?

What if, despite your best endeavours, things go wrong? For example, you judge that the patient is capable of making an informed decision, has been properly informed, and withholds consent. You act in accordance with these wishes, and the outcome is a disaster — the patient suffers in ways that could have been avoided and then complains of having been neglected. Or you decide that the patient is not capable of giving consent, so you act in the way that you genuinely think will be in his or her best interests, but, again, it turns out to be a disaster.

What are your moral responsibilities, and what should you do?

A generally accepted view is that, provided you have decided carefully and impartially, and on the basis of as much evidence as you could, you have then fulfilled your moral obligation. If the results of your decision do not turn out as your evidence indicated, you are not morally at fault. Although your decision has unwittingly brought about the awful consequences and you are *causally* responsible for them, you are not *culpably* responsible.

No moral blame attaches to you, because people cannot be morally responsible for consequences they could not have anticipated at the time of making their decision, so you have no reason to accuse yourself of moral failure. Indeed, it is your moral duty not to agonise in this way, since to do so may deflect your attention from new situations which need your best professional consideration and judgement. What you should do, however, is review what happened in order to avoid the same thing happening again.

References

Beauchamp, T.L. and Childress, J.F. (1989) *Principles of Biomedical Ethics* (3rd edn.). New York, Oxford University Press.

Bentham, J. (1789) *In An Introduction to the Principles of Morals and Legislation.* Burns, J.H. and Hart, H.L.A. (eds.) (1982) London, Methuen.

Cohen, D.R. and Henderson, J.B. (1988) *Health Prevention and Economics.* Oxford, Oxford University Press.

Dimond, B. (1990) *Legal Aspects of Nursing.* Hemel Hempstead, Prentice Hall.

Hare, R.M. (1981) *Moral Thinking.* Oxford, Clarendon.

Kant, I. (1785) *Groundwork of the Metaphysics of Morals*, translated by H.J. Paton (1948) as *The Moral Law*. London, Hutchinson.

National Health Service (1990) *A Guide to Consent for Examination or Treatment* (HC(90)22). London, Department of Health.

The Patient's Charter (1991) London, HMSO.

Tschudin, V. (1991) *Counselling Skills for Nurses* (3rd edn.). London, Baillière Tindall.

Weinman, J. (1987) *An Outline of Psychology as Applied to Medicine* (2nd edn.). Bristol, Wright.

Further Reading

Beauchamp, T.L. and Childress, J.F. (1989) The principle of respect for autonomy. In *Principles of Biomedical Ethics* (3rd edn.), New York, Oxford University Press.

Pages 74–79, in particular, on informed consent. Discussion includes competence, disclosure of information, understanding by patients, non–coercion, voluntariness, etc.

Faden, R.R. and Beauchamp, T.L. (1986) *A History and Theory of Informed Consent*. New York, Oxford University Press.

An extensive study of informed consent.

Faulder, C. (1985). *Whose Body is it? The Troubling Issue of Informed Consent*. London, Virago.

A discussion emphasising the patient's perspective.

Gillon, R. (1985) Autonomy and consent. In Lockwood, M. (ed) *Moral Dilemmas in Modern Medicine*, Oxford, Oxford University Press.

Harris, J. (1989) *The Value of Life*, London, Routledge.

Discusses informed consent in the context of respect for persons, the obligation to inform and paternalism.

CHAPTER 3

Advocacy

Diane Marks-Maran

Advocacy is about individual choice. As such it is about human values: promoting them, upholding them and identifying them.
This chapter looks at advocacy from a number of different perspectives, each by a different proponent. This gives the subject a new angle, as these perspectives are compared for their strengths and possible weak points. Through such an analysis nurses can begin to clarify their own values about nursing and their relationships with patients or clients.

Introduction

The term *'advocacy'* is one which is increasingly appearing in the nursing literature, and it is becoming a common assumption that being an advocate for the patient is part of the nurse's role.

This chapter will attempt to explore advocacy by examining its definitions and by critically reviewing a number of perspectives of advocacy.

The notion of advocacy is linked to the ethical principle of individual freedom, a principle which is not necessarily easy to define. A phrase commonly heard among nurses is 'I had no choice. I had to do . . .' Yet, in reality, if we see ourselves as autonomous beings, there is always choice, and perhaps the phrase 'I had no choice' is really a way of saying that, for whatever reason, 'I'm doing something because it is easier to do so than not to do so'. The consequences are more manageable. The difference between the phrase 'I had no choice', and 'I choose to do . . .' is that the latter recognises freedom of choice and

autonomy while the former denies individual freedom of choice and autonomy. Advocacy, if it is to exist, begins with a belief in the principle of individual freedom and choice. If nurses do not see themselves as autonomous individuals with freedom of choice in nursing, then they will be unable to act as advocates for patients.

Advocacy Defined

One of the problems in finding clear definitions for terms like 'advocacy' and 'advocate' has been highlighted by Johnstone (1989). She points out that modern definitions of 'advocacy' and 'advocate' refer to courtroom situations. Johnstone warns that although the legal sense of the word 'advocacy' is one which is popularly used, it is not necessarily the only way to define advocacy, nor should it be that lawyers have a monopoly on the term's usage.

It is understandable that the modern usage of the word 'advocate' has legal connotations. The earliest origin of the word, dating back to 14th century France, is the word *avocat* (French) or *advocatus* (Latin), both of which refer to someone who is summoned or called to aid the cause of another in a court of justice. The Oxford English Dictionary (Murray 1986) defines an advocate as:

1) One whose profession it is to plead the cause of anyone in a court of justice. . .

2) One who pleads, intercedes, or speaks for, or on behalf of, another . . . a pleader, intercessor, defender. . .

3) One who defends, maintains, publically recommends . . . on behalf of a proposal or tenet. . .

The above definitions help to explain why the modern usage of the words 'advocate' and 'advocacy' have courtroom connotations. However, it can also be argued that the above definitions can point nurses in the direction of the *intention* of advocacy without being restricted by the legal context of the common usage of the word advocacy.

Johnstone (1989) might hold the key to defining advocacy in a nursing (rather than legal) context when she says that the question which remains is what definition of advocacy nurses should adopt (if at all) in their attempts to uphold important *human values* in the health care context.

The legal definitions of 'advocate' and 'advocacy' refer to legal issues and responsibilities. If advocacy is to be a role for nurses, then nurses need to find moral definitions which examine the role of nurses in upholding moral (rather than legal) responsibility and human values. Johnstone also challenges nurses to:

assess whether a non-legal sense of the term [advocacy] would necessarily offer nurses the tool they are seeking to explain and strengthen the philosophical basis of the nurse–patient relationship.

The remainder of this chapter will attempt to examine the perspectives of a number of nursing authors on advocacy and how these perspectives offer suggestions as to what (if any) role nurses might have as advocates for patients in the light of the following example.

Case history

- Mrs B was a 45-year-old teacher. Four years ago she had a mastectomy for carcinoma of the breast. This was followed by a course of radiotherapy. A year ago bone and lung metastases were treated with chemotherapy. This had been a traumatic time for Mrs B; she suffered much with nausea, vomiting and diarrhoea, and also lost her hair. Her present admission was due to liver metastases and ascites.

  Mrs B and her family knew that her life was fore-shortened and they had spent the last year together 'putting things in order'. Mrs B and the family had together decided that she would not accept any further treatments. She had told the consultant of this decision, and had also stated it as a foregone conclusion when she was admitted.

  When the consultant visited her he did not say much, but simply wrote on the prescription chart that a central line should be inserted for total parenteral nutrition.

Imagine yourself as the nurse caring for Mrs B.

Patricia Benner

Benner (1984) equates excellence in clinical nursing with advocacy. She suggests that excellence requires commitment and involvement, which are two key requirements for advocacy as well. Her understanding of advocacy is based on the concept of power.

Benner points out that nurses believe that the same qualities they need for their caring role are also those qualities which make them powerless in a male-dominated hierarchical health care setting. Nurses are caught up in masculine definitions of power which emphasise competitiveness, domination and control. Medicine is characterised by these concepts. The danger is that nurses, believing that feminine values have kept them and nursing subservient, will believe that the way to stop the problem is to learn to play masculine power games. The expansion of nursing into technical work is an example of this.

Benner suggests that what nurses need to do is adopt a different definition or understanding of power. They need to move away from the masculine definition of power (competitiveness, domination, control) to a feminine (caring) definition. In redefining power from such a feminine (caring) perspective, nurses use their caring power to *empower* patients, not to dominate, coerce or control them. By empowering their clients, nurses do not dominate, but care. Benner identified certain qualities of caring (feminine) power which she observed in her study of excellence in clinical nursing. These qualities are:

- transformative power;

- integrative caring;

- advocacy;

- healing power;

- participative/affirmative power;

- problem-solving.

The focus here is on the third of these as being relevant to seeking non-legal explanations or definitions of advocacy.

Benner describes advocacy using an interesting term

from American football. She says 'patients and families frequently need the nurse to *run defence* for them'.

The term 'running defence' in American football describes the team's attempt to enable the person carrying the football to run down the field and score, other players running alongside the ball carrier to prevent the opposition from tackling or stopping him. Those players running alongside the ball carrier are 'running defence'. It is an interesting analogy, where the patient or family is the ball carrier, moving towards the goal. The nurse is running defence — not interfering with the patient or family, not deciding what or where the goal is, but merely preventing other things from interfering with the patient. Examples of things which may stop the patient from reaching his or her goal are medical jargon and fear, both of which can block the patient's ability to understand what is going on around him or her.

In the exercise of advocacy, according to Benner, the nurse's role is to remove obstacles, stand alongside and enable the patient to reach the goal through being empowered.

In the example given above, the nurse as advocate is aware of power: the doctor's (male) power of competition. His is a competition with life, and he attempts to win. The nurse's (feminine) powerlessness would make her carry out his prescription without question. The nurse's new (feminine) power — which is caring — leads her to empower the patient. This does not consist of interfering, but of helping the patient to decide for herself.

Benner, therefore, sees advocacy as more than just an 'add on' role of the nurse. She places advocacy within a well-argued philosophical basis (feminine v masculine understanding of power). She attempts (although mainly superficially) to defend the need for patient advocacy in health care settings. Benner does not put forward any arguments for or against advocacy as being uniquely placed within nursing but she does place advocacy as a component of excellence in caring.

Finally, Benner does begin to identify the circumstances in which nurses might fulfil their role as advocates to patients. One strength of Benner's arguments is that she equates advocacy with redefined definitions of power and excellence in nursing practice, arguing that the focus of the caring (feminine) perspective of power lies in the strength of the nurse–patient relationship.

Leah Curtin

Curtin (1986) made the point that the purpose of nursing is the welfare of other human beings and that this purpose is not a scientific end but rather a moral one. This is an interesting, if not provocative statement, suggesting that nursing is not a science but, rather, a moral art.

The reason for this, according to Curtin, is that nursing is derived from the involvement of nurses with patients, the relationship nurses have with patients and the promotion in that relationship of what is mutually seen (by nurse and patient) as *good*.

Curtin argues that when a person is threatened by the effects of illness and disability there is a need to protect the humanity of the sufferer. She moves away from both the patients' rights and legal concepts of advocacy and proposes an alternative definition and understanding of advocacy, which she refers to as 'human advocacy'. In doing this, she attempts to erase the boundary between nurse and patient by suggesting that we are all involved in a common humanity with common needs and common human rights which nurses and patients share.

It is this *common humanity* which gives rise to the need for human beings to act as advocates for each other. What Curtin is suggesting is that because we are joined together in common humanity, this commonality compels nurses to accept human advocacy as the basis of the nurse–patient relationship.

Curtin argues that nurses are best placed to take on the human advocacy role because of the sustained amount of time which nurses spend providing intimate physical and emotional care. In defining the role of the nurse in human advocacy, Curtin suggests that this means creating 'an atmosphere that is open to, and supportive of the individual's decision making'. Curtin also describes advocacy as 'as natural as living and dying'. In critically appraising Curtin's notion of advocacy, it could be suggested that her statement that there are no 'patient's rights' but only human rights, is a strong argument. In the same way, advocacy being 'natural' is a strong argument. However, her suggestion, that because nurses spend so much time with patients, undertaking intimate and emotional care, they are uniquely placed to act as human advocates, is a weak argument.

Johnstone (1989) argues that no one nurse actually spends so much time with any one patient as to be uniquely placed to gain intimate knowledge of the patient. Johnstone reminds us that even in the outside world two people can live together for years and still not know the kinds of health care choice each would be likely to make in times of illness. If indeed, as Curtin puts forward, human advocacy is derived from common humanity, common needs and common human rights, then any human being (doctor, nurse, lay person) is uniquely placed to act as an advocate for another.

If the nurse in the example given acts as an advocate in the style put forward by Curtin, she needs to be aware of the common humanity of all concerned. This means being aware of common needs and common human rights.

If all individuals are to be treated in terms of human

needs, each has to state his or her needs. The patient must state her needs to have her wishes not to receive further treatments respected. The doctor must state his need to act according to his professional duty to save life. The nurse must state the need to work with both in such a way that keeps her integrity. The common human rights then are rights to be listened to and heard: rights to be respected as individuals, and rights to self-determination.

The nurse, conscious of her role as advocate, must highlight these needs and rights. Once this is done, decisions will be possible.

With regard to critically evaluating the extent to which Curtin clarifies the circumstances under which nurses can fulfil their role as advocates, certain concerns must be highlighted. Curtin claims that human advocacy is 'as *natural* as living and dying'. This presupposes an innate ability and skill to take on this role. In moral terms, Curtin is attempting to describe human advocacy as natural, but this does not address the range of skills required to take on the role satisfactorily, that is, skills which are learned, rather than being innate.

Sally Gadow

Gadow (1983) attempts to provide a philosphical foundation for nursing by making the claim that existential advocacy is the philosophical basis for nursing.

Gadow rejects what she calls the 'consumer advocacy' model embodied in the patient's rights movement as well as the paternalistic advocacy approach. Hers is an existential approach, echoed by Gilligan (1982, 1987) who points out that the ethics of care and responsibility differ from the ethics of rights and justice.

Gadow believes that the most fundamental and valuable human right is the right to *self-determination*. For Gadow, existential advocacy is about engaging in activities which actively assist individuals to exercise their freedom of self-determination. When individuals are unable to exercise their freedom of self-determination, their wholeness — their integrity — as persons is compromised. The underlying assumption behind existential advocacy, according to Gadow, is *not* about what individuals should want to do, nor is it about safeguarding individuals' rights to do what they want. Rather, it is about helping people to become clear about what they want to do. The advocate's role is to help individuals clarify values in a situation and reach decisions which reflect their values. This, according to Gadow, is the only way a person's decision can be self-determined rather than determined by others.

The nurse caring for Mrs B has, if she uses Gadow's model of advocacy, to be aware of the right to self-determination. She does not tell the patient what to think or do, but helps her to clarify her own situation.

The nurse as advocate should therefore help the patient first of all to clarify her own values. What are her values with regard to life, death, suffering, illness? How does she value these things? How does her family value them when applied to her?

The role of the nurse is to spend time with the patient going through a process of value-clarification. This is the only way in which self-determination becomes clear. This demands that the nurse has extensive skills of inter-personal communication and counselling, that the nurse is aware of her skills, and that she is able to use them when the need arises.

Johnstone (1989) questions whether or not Gadow can justify that self-determination is *the* most valuable human right. A second concern is the degree to which nurses are able to act in such a way as to enable others to clarify values and make authentic and self-determined choices without unknowingly manipulating that choice.

Kath Melia

Melia (1989) begins her arguments about advocacy by making the point that nurses, like all other professionals, cannot remove the fact that they have power in the nurse–patient relationship. Although Melia does not define power, as Benner does, it seems obvious that Melia is referring to Benner's masculine definitions of power. Melia also appears to subscribe to the legal definition of advocacy rather than attempting to find alternative definitions. She believes that in taking on an advocacy role, nurses take on a role similar to that of a barrister in court. This, she argues, nurses cannot do; therefore nurses cannot really be advocates. Melia seems to equate advocacy with nurses standing 'up for what they see as the patient's rights'. This legalistic interpretation of advocacy, not subscribed to by Benner, Curtin or Gadow, makes of advocacy an unattractive form of paternalism.

Melia also states that the ethical arguments to support the advocacy role in nursing have to do with rights and obligations. Her concept of advocacy is legalistic, whereas others (Curtin 1986, Gadow 1983, Benner 1984, Gilligan 1982, 1987) would argue that ethical concepts, such as caring, responsibility and self-determination, offer alternatives to the rights and obligations arguments.

It is clear that Melia believes that advocacy is a role outside the nurse's competence and the nurse–patient relationship. However, in critically evaluating her arguments for this point of view, several things become clear. Melia does not seek to find an alternative to the legalistic definition of advocacy. Therefore, although there is a strong legal argument against the role of the nurse as an advocate, the moral and philosophical argument put forward — that nurses have power in the nurse–patient relationship — is weak. Melia also does not attempt to argue whether there is a role for *anyone* to act as patient's advocate in health care contexts, unless a legal opinion is required.

Like Jonstone (1989) who expressed concern with Curtin's (1986) suggestion that nurses are uniquely placed to be advocates for the patient because of the amount of time spent with the patient, Melia suggests that it is hard for anyone really to know what the patient sees as his or her best interests.

Following this thesis, the nurse in the example given cannot act as an advocate in any practical way.

Mary Kohnke

Kohnke (1982) offers one of the most simple alternatives to the legal definition of advocacy. She states that the role of the nurse advocate is simply to *inform* and *support* patients in whatever decision they make. Kohnke offers quite concise definitions of *informing* and *supporting*.

Informing is described as supplying patients with the information they need to make informed decisions. However, Kohnke says that before taking on this role, nurses need to think through the following:

- Do they want to take on the role of advocate?

- Do they want clients to have information which was previously undisclosed?

- Do they understand what it will mean personally to disclose the information?

- Are they certain that they have the most up-to-date, relevant information?

Supporting consists of undertaking two roles: an action role and a non-action role. Kohnke describes the action role as, firstly, assuring patients that they have both the right and responsibility to make their own choices and, secondly, reassuring patients that they do not have to be influenced by pressure from anyone to change their decision.

When this is applied to the nurse in the example, the scenario is as follows.

- The nurse is aware of two main tasks; informing and supporting. In the task of informing the patient she has to ask herself four questions:

    (i) Does she want to take on the role of advocate here? — Yes.

    (ii) Does she have information which the patient is unaware of but should also have? — Yes.

    (iii) Does the nurse know that she might cause conflict between the patient and the consultant, and between the consultant and herself? — Yes.

    (iv) Does the nurse know that she has the correct information? — Yes.

- The nurse therefore informs Mrs B of the directive to insert a central line for nutrition.

- She then goes on to assure Mrs B that she can and must decide for herself whether she will accept this treatment.

This is the nurse's action role. She then supports Mrs B further by stating that Mrs B should not feel that she is being pressurised by anyone in her decision. This is the nurse's non-action role. In the words of Gadow, the nurse describes self-determination.

In this process the nurse has also to apply a measure of self-awareness in that she needed to ask herself further, 'Am I rescuing this patient?' Rescuing, Kohnke states emphatically, is not part of advocacy.

The non-action role requires the nurse consciously to refrain from subtly undermining a patient's decision. Kohnke suggests that the nurse advocate must take care not to move into a rescuing role, eg fighting the patient's battles for him.

The philosophical basis of Kohnke's definition or description of the nurse advocate is as follows. Firstly, all individuals have a right to self-determination. Secondly, Kohnke claims that ethics and professional codes do not protect the patient's right to self-determination. Thirdly, ethics, according to Kohnke, encourages nurses to act as rescuers to patients — to make decisions for them — while advocacy is merely the process of informing people so that they can make decisions and then supporting them in whatever decision they make.

The unique contributions to the advocacy debate from Kohnke are these: that ethics cannot teach us the role of advocacy and that advocacy acts as a bridge between the moral and the legal, ensuring that the legal requirements for information are met as is the moral requirement of honouring the right to self-determination. Johnstone (1989), however, warns that this claim can be seriously misleading and dangerous by ignoring the role that ethics and morality play in the law.

As a counter-argument to Johnstone it is possible to say that what is legally right and what is morally right can be very different. However, it is questionable as to whether or not advocacy bridges that gap.

Kohnke differs greatly from Curtin and rejects the notion that advocacy is something natural, suggesting rather that advocacy is a learned skill and an acquired role and one which the nurse chooses to take on. This is in keeping with Kohnke's belief in self-determination. The nurse determines whether to undertake this role and whether he or she has the knowledge, skill and personal qualities to take on the advocacy role.

One strength of Kohnke's work is that she identifies the risks and hazards of taking on the role of advocate.

Carroll Quinn and Michael Smith

Quinn and Smith (1987) and Smith (1980) attempt to use the concept of advocacy to define the *relationship* between nursing and human autonomy.

Smith (1980) identifies different roles which nurses take on in their relationships with patients, two of which have relevance in our discussions here: the nurse as a surrogate mother and the nurse as an advocate.

The nurse as surrogate mother proposes a particular way of providing care. In this role, the nurse's definition of care is embodied in the phrase 'to take care of'. The nurse acts supposedly in the patient's best interests, but the relationship is a mother–child relationship with the nurse exercising a duty 'to take care of' and the patient acting in a dependent role. The word 'paternalism' (or 'parentalism') best describes this relationship. Autonomy and self-determination are not part of the surrogate mother role.

The nurse as advocate is based on a philosophy of professional patient care (Quinn and Smith 1987). Advocacy recognises that patients are independent and that the nurse has an obligation to respect the patient's autonomy while at the same time providing care. The key to this lies in redefining 'providing care'. In the surrogate mother role, care is described as 'taking care of'. In the advocate role, the nurse 'cares for' the patient.

Mayeroff (1972) describes 'caring for' as follows:

> to care for another person, in the most significant sense, is to help him grow and actualise himself

To enable this to happen requires from the nurse a recognition of what the patient is striving for, and the goals and values that the patient considers important. In this context 'caring for' another in the role of advocate always involves respect for the person's own chosen direction.

Quinn and Smith (1987) suggest that all professionals should be advocates and, in doing so, act in a way which respects the autonomy of their clients.

Looking once more at the nurse in the given example, we see that when applying Quinn and Smith's theory of advocacy, the relationship between the nurse and the patient is of crucial importance.

If the nurse takes on the role of surrogate, she takes care of Mrs B. She decides on behalf of Mrs B, treats her as she (the nurse) deems fit and generally (in Kohnke's words) 'rescues' her.

If the nurse decides that the role of advocate is more relevant, then she cares for Mrs B. This care is provided in the way which Mrs B wishes, what is possible and what is right. The yardstick for measuring what is right is the relationship between nurse and patient.

When critically evaluating Quinn and Smith's concept of advocacy, it is seen that they do not make explicit the criteria for determining what an advocate is. The difference between 'to take care of' and 'to care for' is a useful distinction to describe the differences between the surrogate and advocate roles but the philosophical basis for this is less clear. It is possible to argue that 'caring for' could be just as paternalistic as 'taking care of'. Perhaps a third definition of care — 'to care about' — is more appropriate to the advocacy role than 'to care for'.

Quinn and Smith do not attempt to describe what the role of the advocate is. Like Curtin, they argue that nurses are uniquely placed to take on the role of advocate because of their intimate contact with patients and because they are seen as less authoritarian than doctors.

Both these arguments, however, are weak. Although

nurses are seen as less authoritarian than doctors, they can still hold positions of power (in the masculine sense) over patients, as Benner points out.

One strength of Quinn and Smith is their belief that the skills of listening and empathy are required of the nurse advocate, implying, like Kohnke, that these are learned qualities. Quinn and Smith raise a unique and legitimate question: Do nurses have the authority to act as patients' advocate'? Benner (1984) would argue that authority (or power) in its masculine definition (domination, control, competitiveness) is not in the hands of nurses but that authority (power) in the feminine or caring context is what nursing is all about.

Conclusions

This chapter has attempted to provide a broad overview and critical analysis of advocacy. Several different perspectives on advocacy have been put forward providing diverse philosophical and practical explanations. It seems clear that as we seek to decide whether or not there is an advocacy role for the nurses and what, if at all, that role is to be, each of us must begin by clarifying our own values about nursing and the nurse–patient relationship. It is only then that we will be in a position to decide where advocacy fits into our value system. Advocacy, like the Nursing Process, is not just another set of tasks to do for patients. It is a way of being. For this reason, nursing needs to seek alternative perspectives to the legal approach to explaining advocacy and in doing so place advocacy within a total value system of caring.

However, in making decisions about our role as patient advocates — if we are to have such a role — we perhaps need to return to the ethical principle of *freedom*. At the beginning of this chapter the point was made that advocacy is linked to this principle. In order to take on an advocacy role, nurses may first need to examine the extent to which they exercise freedom of choice in their nursing practice. The extent to which nurses see themselves as autonomous and accountable practitioners, who exercise professional choice in day-to-day practice, will be the extent to which they can act as advocates for the patient.

References

Benner, P. (1984) *From Novice to Expert: Power and Excellence in Nursing Practice.* Menlo Park, Addison Wesley.

Curtin, L. (1986) The nurse as advocate: a philosophical foundation for nursing. In Chinn (ed.), *Ethical Issues in Nursing,* Rockville, Md, Aspen.

Gadow, S. (1983) Existential advocacy: philosophical foundation of nursing. In Murphy and Hunter (eds.), *Ethical Problems in the Nurse Patient Relationship,* Boston, Allen & Bacon.

Gilligan, C. (1982) *In a Different Voice: Psychological Theory and Women's Development.* Cambridge, Mass, Harvard University Press.

Gilligan, C. (1987) Moral orientation and moral development. In Kittay and Meyers (eds.), *Women and Moral Theory,* New York, Savage, Rowan & Littlefield.

Johnstone, M-J. (1989) *Bioethics, a Nursing Perspective.* Sydney, W.B. Saunders.

Kohnke, M. (1982) *Advocacy: Risk and Reality.* St Louis, C.V. Mosby.

Mayeroff, M. (1972) *On Caring.* New York, Harper & Row.

Melia, K. (1989) *Everyday Ethics.* Edinburgh, Churchill Livingstone.

Murray, J.A.H. (ed.) (1986) *Oxford English Dictionary.* Oxford, Oxford University Press.

Quinn, C, and Smith, M. (1987) *The Professional Commitment: Issues and Ethics in Nursing.* Philadelphia, W.B. Saunders.

Smith, S. (1980) Three models of the nurse-patient relationship. In Spicker and Gadow (eds.), *Images and Ideals,* New York, Springer.

CHAPTER 4

Responsibilities and Rights

Verena Tschudin

One person's rights are another person's responsibilities. What this means in actual practice however, is, not always so clearly definable.

Codes of practice guide nurses in the direction of their duties to patients, colleagues and the wider society. A nurse has professional responsibilities, but personal and moral aspects guide an individual just as much. There are no clear boundaries, making for difficulties and also for challenges to view this subject in a broader sense.

Introduction

One person's rights are another person's responsibilities or duties.

Many people today are very aware of their rights, or what they consider to be their rights. Perhaps it is more difficult to see how responsibilities can be established to fit the rights, and perhaps the personal commitment thus demanded is not always welcome. Two hundred years ago the opposite would have been true in ethical circles when Kant established his theory of Duty Ethics or Deontology. The main feature of this approach was that a citizen 'ought' to act rightly, based on certain personal or societal rules and moral ideals. With the pendulum having swung in the opposite direction, finding a middle path is challenging.

In order to take up this challenge and relate it to nursing in this chapter, it is possible to start with responsibilities, as they are enshrined in some nursing Codes.

International Council of Nurses: Code for Nurses (1973). Reprinted with the permission of the International Council of Nurses

The fundamental responsibility of the nurse is fourfold: to promote health, to prevent illness, to restore health, and to alleviate suffering.

The need for nursing is universal. Inherent in nursing is respect for life, dignity and the rights of man. It is unrestricted by considerations of nationality, race, creed, colour, age, sex, politics or social status.

Nurses render health services to the individual, the family and the community, and coordinate their services with those of related groups.

Nurses and people
The nurse's primary responsibility is to those people who require nursing care.

The nurse, in providing care, respects the beliefs, values and customs of the individual.

The nurse holds in confidence personal information and uses judgement in sharing this information.

Nurses and practice
The nurse carries personal responsibility for nursing practice and for maintaining competence by continual learning.

The nurse maintains the highest standard of nursing care possible within the reality of a specific situation.

The nurse uses judgement in relation to individual competence when accepting and delegating responsibilities.

The nurse when acting in a professional capacity should at all times maintain standards of personal conduct that would reflect credit upon the profession.

Nurses and society
The nurse shares with other citizens the responsibility for initiating and supporting action to meet the health and social needs of the public.

Nurses and co-workers
The nurse sustains a cooperative relationship with co-workers in nursing and other fields.

The nurse takes appropriate action to safeguard the individual when his care is endangered by a co-worker or any other person.

Nurses and the profession
The nurse plays the major role in determining and implementing desirable standards of nursing practice and nursing education.

The nurse is active in developing a core of professional knowledge.

The nurse, acting through the professional organisation, participates in establishing and maintaining equitable social and economic working conditions in nursing.

Code of Professional Conduct for the Nurse, Midwife and Health Visitor (1992). Extract reprinted with the permission of the UKCC

Each registered nurse, midwife, and health visitor shall act, at all times, in such a manner as to:

- safeguard and promote the interests of individual patients and clients;

- serve the interests of society;

- justify public trust and confidence and

- uphold and enhance the good standing and reputation of the professions.

As a registered nurse, midwife or health visitor, you are personally accountable for your practice and, in the exercise of your professional accountability, must:

1 act always in such a manner as to promote and safeguard the interests and well-being of patients and clients;

2 ensure that no action or omission on your part, or within your sphere of responsibility, is detrimental to the interests, condition or safety of patients and clients;

3 maintain and improve your professional knowledge and competence;

4 acknowledge any limitations in your knowledge and competence and decline any duties or responsibilities unless able to perform them in a safe and skilled manner;

5 work in an open and co-operative manner with patients, clients and their families, foster their independence and recognise and respect their involvement in the planning and delivery of care;

6 work in a collaborative and co-operative manner with health care professionals and others involved in providing care, and recognise and respect their particular contributions within the care team;

7 recognise and respect the uniqueness and dignity of each patient and client, and respond to their need for care, irrespective of their ethnic origin, religious beliefs, personal attributes, the nature of their health problems or any other factor;

8 report to an appropriate person or authority, at the earliest possible time, any conscientious objection which may be relevant to your professional practice;

9 avoid any abuse of your privileged relationship with patients and clients and of the privileged access allowed to their person, property, residence or workplace;

10 protect all confidential information concerning patients and clients obtained in the course of professional practice and make disclosures only with consent, where required by the order of a court or where you can justify disclosure in the wider public interest;

11 report to an appropriate person or authority, having regard to the physical, psychological and social effects on patients and clients, any circumstances in the environment of care which could jeopardise standards of practice;

12 report to an appropriate person or authority any circumstances in which safe and appropriate care for patients and clients cannot be provided;

13 report to an appropriate person or authority where it appears that the health or safety of colleagues is at risk, as such circumstances may compromise standards of practice and care;

14 assist professional colleagues, in the context of your own knowledge, experience and sphere of responsibility, to develop their professional competence, and assist others in the care team, including informal carers, to contribute safely and to a degree appropriate to their roles;

15 refuse any gift, favour or hospitality from patients or clients currently in your care which might be interpreted as seeking to exert influence to obtain preferential consideration and

16 ensure that your registration status is not used in the promotion of commercial products or services, declare any financial or other interests in relevant organisations providing such goods or services and ensure that your professional judgement is not influenced by any commercial considerations.

- 'Victoria' was a typical Nightingale ward in a big teaching hospital, with the kitchen and store rooms at one end, and the sluice and fire escape at the other. It was a women's medical ward, but two three-bedded side-rooms by the entrance to the ward were often allocated to men patients. The ward had not been upgraded for a long time as the whole block was due for renovation in a year or two. Some of the equipment was fairly basic and doors and windows testified to an era when fresh air was thought to be essential to survival.

The day had been hectic, with several admissions. One of the side-rooms had become empty and three women from the main ward were moved into it with their belongings and lockers. At 19.00 hrs two men were announced for emergency admission. The evening shift was short of one nurse, and one of the student nurses was there on her first allocation. A staff nurse, just qualified, was in charge.

The admission of two men meant having to move patients again. Two of the women who were moved into the side-room in the morning were asked to go back into the ward, and the third was found a bed on the ward above. This caused an enormous amount of traffic up and down the ward with beds and bags and lockers. The two spaces nearest the sluice were not popular with patients or staff, but that was where the women had to be put — for better or worse.

The night shift began at 21.30 hrs and the three nurses who came on duty found 'Victoria' still looking like Piccadilly Circus: equipment everywhere and nothing moving very fast.

A tutor had made an appointment with the student nurse just starting the night shift, to be with her for an hour or so and help to orient her to the patients and their diagnoses. She too walked into the chaos.

Instead of sitting down with the student, the tutor was soon helping with the situation and answering some bells. She gave out one or two bedpans, and this meant going to the sluice. As she walked towards it she noticed a patient curled up in bed with a coat on top of her. She took another look, and saw that several patients had their coats on their beds.

The part of the ward by the sluice was indeed very cold, with the windows not shutting properly, and it *was* a very cold winter's night.

The tutor went to one patient and commented on the coat. She heard that none of these patients had blankets because they were needed for the new admissions. They all had only one pillow and had made themselves as comfortable as they could by rolling up their spare nightclothes into pillows and using any other clothing to keep warm. All the same, it promised to be a chilly and disturbed night for the women on 'Victoria'.

(The name and details have been changed to disguise the location.)

The Nurse's Legal Responsibility

The ICN Code sees the nurse's professional responsibility as being related to the actual work of health care. The nurse's responsibility can also be seen from another angle — relating to society, to the profession itself, to colleagues and to patients. The fourfold responsibilities of the ICN Code are reflected in the fourfold spheres of influence of individual nurses. Within the spheres, the type of responsibility seen can be described as being legal, personal and moral in character. These will be considered in turn here, relating them to the Codes of Conduct, and to the story of 'Victoria' ward.

One of the hallmarks of a profession is that it trains its own practitioners. In this way the profession controls its teaching and its practice. While nurses were being taught by doctors, the doctors could demand obedience. Now that nurses train nurses, they regulate their own standards. They use their wits, not their obedience, in the care they give, and in the standards and practices they teach and regulate. It can therefore be said that nurses impose their own responsibility by the way they choose to work. This implies that the standards of education and practice are maintained at a constant level and improvements in that level are made by research. A profession which carries out its own research is truly a practitioner-led profession, which has clearly happened in nursing in the last two decades.

A body which trains its own practitioners also has to have a mechanism for ensuring that the standard of practice is maintained. A Register of practitioners has to exist and a body has to be in place to oversee the affairs of the profession. These are the people who set certain standards of education and practice and exercise these by admitting members to and dismissing them from the register according to the standards set.

A Code of Practice is the visible instrument of the maintenance of standards. Such a Code puts forward certain values by which the profession can be measured, both by its own practitioners and by those it serves.

A regulatory body legitimises a profession. This shows that a professional person is responsible both to the profession itself and to society as a whole. Since it is the members of society who are to be its clients, society wants to ensure that when it comes into contact with that profession, everything is as 'user-friendly' as possible or, as the UKCC Code puts it, 'public trust and confidence' are justified.

The professional's responsibility is expressed in accountability (see chapter 5) to the various levels of managerial and regulatory structures. A clearly-defined hierarchy is thought to be helpful in that everybody in the line of command knows their sphere of responsibility and accountability. (It will be seen later that this may not always be the case.)

A nurse's legal responsibilities are therefore seen to be very diverse. Nurses are occasionally heard to say that all they want to do is care for people and not get involved with anything else, especially anything political. Yet since most nurses' posts are approved by officials and managers who may not have any understanding of nurses' professional practice, it could be said that all nurses have to be politically (not necessarily party-politically) aware and active. It is not only a question of defending their own practice, but of respecting the personal and political rights of their patients and clients by upholding standards of practice and also ethical and personal standards and values. This may not always have been understood as a nurse's responsibility, but promoting health, preventing illness and alleviating suffering must be seen as responsibilities within a wide social setting.

The story of 'Victoria' ward highlights the practical failure of many of these points. One of the most obvious difficulties any nurse faces is that the gap between what is taught and what is practised is often very wide. No college or university teaches that patients are frequently obliged to live through chaos on the wards. With constant demands made on nurses by admissions and juggling with space, the best-planned care will suffer. To what extent should a nurse allow this to happen? When does a nurse say that what is happening is contrary to any Code of Conduct, any responsibility, any teaching and indeed any human instinct?

Hannah (1991) believes that the fundamental 'duty of care' which 'the practitioner . . . owes to the client, customer, patient or anyone else [is] a duty not to harm or injure. The duty may go further so as in certain circumstances not to cause economic harm or loss'.

It could be argued that on 'Victoria' ward nobody was either harmed or injured — not physically anyway. The lack of blankets in the ward's coldest corner on the year's coldest night could possibly lead to respiratory tract infections, but the patients were resourceful and guarded against that. However, did not Florence Nightingale herself say that 'hospitals should do the patients no harm'? It is not simply a question of harm or not, but of basic human care, which sees 'comfort' as essential to living.

The nurses' responsibility in this story was not only the legal one of not harming the patients by providing blankets, but was also political in that they needed to know how to use that lever in order to get hold of blankets, or what action to take to ensure that this sort of state did not occur again.

Their responsibility here to society and its members was that such a situation should ideally, due to good, caring, responsible and preventive practice, not have happened. But since such situations are always going to happen, the evaluations made and lessons drawn from them — the accountability — are such that society can trust that good has come out of it. Accountability means that many more situations like those on that ward become public and are scrutinised. This not only highlights the patients' rights, but also helps individual nurses and nursing as a whole to see responsibility in a positive light.

In the terms of the UKCC Code, Clauses 1, 2, 11, 12 and 13 were seriously infringed in this situation. Clause 11 is particularly significant here. To care for people is also to care for their environment. This may sometimes mean taking 'political' action as well as directly giving care. Nurses should not 'tolerate in silence any matters in [their] work setting that place patients at risk, jeopardise standards of practice, or deny patients privacy and dignity' (UKCC 1989). Legal, personal and moral responsibility all join here in caring, promoting health, raising standards, and most importantly, respecting and enhancing the humanity of individuals.

It is not possible to separate responsibility and accountability: they overlap and depend on each other. As the concept of accountability has increasingly been emphasised in recent times, the concept and practice of it have to be understood better by all nurses, and therefore a whole chapter (chapter 5) is dedicated to accountability. Readers should refer to it in conjunction with this one on responsibility.

The Nurse's Personal Responsibility

The lofty and broad responsibilities of the ICN Code have become significantly more specific in the UKCC Code. Yet when these are compared with *The Patient's Charter* (see p. 107) the nurse's only obvious responsibility seems to be to wear a name badge!

It is increasingly recognised that the relationship between nurse and patient or client is of paramount importance at every level of health care. The whole concept of caring is built on it. The idea of primary nursing rests on it. Nursing models promote it; and — yes — even the name badge which nurses now should wear points to the fact that two people who relate should do so on a human basis, that is as two persons, not simply as professional and client. The nub therefore is what the relationship is, or is about.

There are several models available for looking at the professional helping relationship, among them Lambourne (1983), Campbell (1984), Veatch (1972) and May (1975). The model by May has some interesting points which can help to clarify the relationship between nurses and patients or clients, and how rights and responsibilities arise.

May (1975) considers the (medical) helping relationship to be characterised either by 'code, covenant, contract, or philanthropy'.

A code, says May, 'is usually categorical and universal . . . it is concerned with appropriate form . . . it is concerned not only with what is done but how it is done . . . it touches on . . . style and decorum . . . [it] eschews

involvement . . . it does not, in and of itself, encourage personal involvement with the patient'. In other words, a code sets limits and particularly emphasises the 'professional' role. Professional and client know where each other's boundaries are and each is exhorted to respect them.

A covenant is something which is exchanged between partners. May (1975) takes the word and the idea from the Bible where covenants are made between God and the Israelites. The covenant usually includes the elements of:

- a gift (God delivered the Israelites from slavery);

- an exchange of promises (the Law given to the Israelites);

- the subsequent life shaped by the gift and the promises.

Covenant ethics and relationships are responsive in character, says May: each depends on the other.

In the words of May's theory, the gift which nurses give is their care and professional expertise. The exchange of promises is to fulfil each other's needs. The patient needs the nurse and the nurse's skill and expertise at a time of need. The nurse also needs the patient: to learn the nursing skill and craft in the first place, to gain a living from it, and constantly to sharpen nursing practice, so gaining satisfaction. However, this is seldom openly acknowledged. Nevertheless, the life or relationship between nurse and patient is based on these two aspects. What this model expresses, therefore, is the idea of responsiveness, that is, each person in a relationship responds to the other's needs and therefore has his or her own needs met.

Chapman (1980) believes that patients have a responsibility to allow nurses to care for them. Thus the dependent patients satisfy one of the nurses' psychological needs.

Whether this is a material (May) or psychological (Chapman) need is not necessarily the point here. What is the point is the need one for the other; one responds to the other's needs. This gives the idea of covenant a much more human aspect. The distance between giver and receiver, professional and client, is considerably narrowed, and what is seen are two people interacting at the point of need.

A contract, May points out, is characterised by informed consent. A contract 'includes an exchange of information on the basis of which an agreement is reached and a subsequent exchange of goods' (or money or services) takes place. A contract 'presupposes that people are primarily governed by self-interest'.

As for philanthropy, May dismisses it as a 'pose' and a 'condescension of charity'. It represents the paternalism — or parentalism — so common in health professionals.

Clearly May favours the covenant relationship as the most useful and helpful one. It is the one which enhances the person most. The relationship between two people at critical moments is increasingly being seen as the main element in ethical decision-making (eg Niebuhr 1963, Noddings 1984), and a better guide than either duty or the greatest good to be achieved.

The responsibilities that nurses have in this context relate to themselves and the person of the patient or client as human beings. What matters is how they express these responsibilities in caring. It is not a question of 'giving is better than receiving'; that would be philanthropy and go against the principle of covenant. But it is a question of responsibility — and response-*ability* — seen within a relationship based on human needs.

The personal responsibility is therefore first and foremost to a *person*, rather than simply to a patient or client. When responsibility is to a client or customer it is characterised by a certain 'professional distance', and in that sense the hierarchy of responsibility has operated adequately, each step representing one further level of responsibility and also one step further away from the person in need. A responsibility based on relationship appears not so much as a line — usually up and/or down — like a ladder, but as concentric circles. All involved with the person are responsible to that person and interact with each other as a team, and are therefore on the same level, not higher or lower down. This should ideally be illustrated in 3-D; as attempted in the following:

Responsibility is circular rather than linear and touches the client at all levels. Circles are more flexible than lines, moving around the client as need demands.

With everyone seeing their responsibility as being to the person of the patient rather than to a manager, the basis of caring would take on a different image.

It is then also possible to exchange that patient with yourself. You can see yourself in the middle of a web of circles all concerned with you. This circle cares for you as a person, supports you, teaches you, helps you. In turn you support, teach and help others. In an equal exchange it is easier to see that personal responsibility has to do with knowing your personal strengths and weaknesses; learning and increasing your knowledge (UKCC Code Clause 3); working not only in a team but also in a community; taking rest and not becoming burnt out; being aware of your values and respecting them; not compromising those values in the course of duty; and being as human as is possible in the circumstances.

To take the story of 'Victoria' ward, this would mean that the nurses might have refused to accept two more admissions as this clearly overstretched their own resources as well as those of their patients. They would have been mindful of the relationship with their patients being of primary importance and would therefore have refused to subject them to conditions which they would not have tolerated for themselves. The tutor would certainly have given a hand, but would have alerted her student to the impossibility of the situation and helped the student to see what were her responsibilities in this situation, so that she in turn could act with integrity, humanity and responsibility. The tutor is then not the philanthropist, but represents just one of the circles around the student (and any patient) which facilitates and enriches.

This is perhaps put in terms of the ideal and the possible rather than what usually happens, but then ethics is about the ideal and the possible in terms of both facts and relationships.

The personal responsibilities highlighted here can now be seen as reflecting the legal responsibilities. What one nurse does on one ward reflects what all nurses do everywhere. Equally, what one nurse neglects to do in one situation, and does not recognise as her personal responsibility, also reflects what society does, accepts, tolerates — or challenges.

The Nurse's Moral Responsibility

Because responsibility is seen as something wider than just duty, it is considered to be covenantal rather than just contractual in character. As a consequence, it is linked to freedom, to goodness and to rightness (Tschudin 1992). It has to do with being responsible, rather than simply having responsibility. Somewhat tongue in cheek someone once said that the best way to avoid responsibility is to say, 'I've got responsibilities'.

The moral responsibility is to oneself, to the person of the patient or client, to colleagues, to the profession and to society at large. It is taking all the aspects of responsibility so far described and making them obvious. A responsible person is one who not only thinks responsibly but also acts responsibly.

In his speech to inaugurate the National Centre for Nursing and Midwifery Ethics in April 1991, Geoff Hunt, the Director of the Centre, outlined the concept of moral responsibility. He said that 'moral responsibility means accepting and carrying the burden of judgement and decision in matters of right and wrong'. This is based on the person's free will and freedom to use that judgement. But he pointedly asked whether nurses *do* in fact have the freedom to judge, decide and act on the basis of their convictions. When that freedom is not present there is less than full moral responsibility. Then in fact there is:

- moral compromise;
- moral incompetence;
- moral weakness;
- moral servitude;
- moral indifference.

Hunt did not set out to say *what* could be done to change these negatives into positives. He did not say that one can be sure whether something is compromise or indifference. Rather, he believed that there is sometimes a blurring

between what may be weakness or even wickedness, between incompetence and impossibility.

Nurses are often not clear what they should do for the best in a situation and then feel guilty for having compromised their own standards and conscience, or the patient or a colleague. It is often totally impossible to know what one can or cannot change. The wisdom to know the difference between them cannot be obtained from a Code, a book or a colleague. It comes with 'being there' and doing what one must do as a human being. Only in acting in the most fitting way is it then possible to say that one acted morally responsibly and ethically right.

In order to provide and restore health, prevent illness, and alleviate suffering, and to foster trust and confidence and safeguard the interests of individual patients and clients, the nurses in the story above needed to have acted morally. They needed to have been aware that they had the moral freedom to fulfil all that society, and the profession and their patients demanded of them and that Codes enshrine in words. Every nurse knows, however, that the constraints put on them make much of that a theory, and not a reality. The saga of the 'Whistleblower' Graham Pink in 1990 and 1991 (Turner 1990) has clearly shown up these difficulties (see also Volume V in this series).

The nurses on 'Victoria' ward would have to promote the patients' rights, become their advocates, take seriously their role as change agents, promote care based on relationships and not on expediency, consider their own needs for and of maintaining health and personal integrity and that of their colleagues, and critically evaluate their environment and that of their patients. All this would be necessary to take their responsibility seriously and promote health at all levels. When that can be done, then the ethical principles of justice and honesty are also regarded, greater good for all is achieved, and life is valued for what it is, not only for what it demands. The moral freedom which makes this possible is then the stimulus to ethical behaviour. To achieve this may however need a few more whistleblowers, and research into the presence or absence of moral responsibility in nurses as persons and nursing as a profession.

The Institution's Responsibilities and Rights

Just as nurses' responsibility is to their patients and clients, so the institution's responsibility is first and foremost to its employees.

Nurses need to be able to carry out their job, and for

that they need to be trained. They need to be able to make professional decisions and for that they need professional autonomy. They also need moral autonomy, and freedom from bureaucratic interference. This is something which is increasingly being seen as important.

The nature of the nurses' job is such that for it to be carried out professionally they need equipment: beds, machinery, sterile packs, etc. These need to be supplied by the hospital or institution. The nurse uses, but the hospital supplies. And what is supplied must be useable: it must be safe, what is needed and in the quantity needed.

The institution also has a duty to pay its staff, on time, the correct amount. It has a duty to supply the staff, and of the correct grades. It has a duty to supply and maintain the environment and make it a safe place to work in. The responsibilities of the institution are mostly legal ones based on contracts, but it is people who carry out orders and maintain the system. How the orders are carried out and the system is maintained depends therefore on these people and their personal sense of responsibility and care. The direct patient contact which nurses have, and which gives them a sense of satisfaction and fulfilment of needs, is not so clear for the army of workers who service the nurses and all those who deal with patients. Theirs is not so obviously a reciprocal relationship. They may not be looking for it in the same way, but their influence is felt at every level. A hospital or institution is quickly noted for its atmosphere. If care and relationships are seen as important, then it matters not only *that* you receive your payslip, but also *how* you receive it. If there is no sense of responsibility to one's fellow human beings other than getting a salary at the end, that somehow filters through the whole institution, and is also felt at the bedside of the patients, however remote they may be from the ultimate managers of the institution.

Last but not least, the policies which an institution

makes and expects to be adhered to, have to be realistic
and workable, and in line with policies and laws in other
institutions.

Besides these responsibilities, the institution has the
right to expect from and demand of its employees that
they carry out their job and work to the best of their
knowledge and ability. It demands that employees make
known any reasons for not fulfilling their duties, such as
in sickness or when they object to any practice which they
consider impossible to carry out (UKCC Code Clause 8).

The story of 'Victoria' ward highlights several of these
points: the blankets which were not available; the building
(doors and windows) which was neglected; the policy of
having disproportionate numbers of men and women on
the same ward which made conditions for patients and
nurses difficult. The institution's responsibilities are here
seen as absent or neglected more than present and correct.
But the nurses also had a duty to report such difficulties
and discrepancies, and it is the institution's right to hear
of them and be able to correct them.

By looking at the institution's responsibilities and rights
together, the bridge is made between the two halves of
this chapter, and rights — of both patients and nurses —
are now considered.

The Patient's Legal Rights

The Human Rights Movement has come into being after
World War II, and has since steadily gained in momen-
tum. The idea of human rights builds on the notion of
basic protection for individuals (Jameton 1984, p. 139)
and is closely allied to legal thinking, aiming to establish
universal standards of justice and making legislation available to enforce these standards (O'Neill 1991).

As with responsibility, there are legal and moral rights.

Rights tend in the first place to be expressed in terms of personal rights ('I have a right to . . .') and therefore the personal aspect of rights will not be emphasised in this section.

The patient's legal rights have been officially published for the first time in Britain in 1991 in *The Patient's Charter*. This document may become the basis for much discussion in health care, with patients citing it in their favour, and nurses blaming it as being unrealistic to fit their resources.

The Patient's Charter
Every citizen has the following National Health Services rights:

- to receive health care on the basis of clinical need, regardless of ability to pay;

- to be registered with a GP;

- to receive emergency medical care at any time, through your GP or the emergency ambulance service and hospital accident and emergency departments;

- to be referred to a consultant, acceptable to you, when your GP thinks it necessary and to be referred for a second opinion if you and your GP agree this is desirable;

- to be given a clear explanation of any treatment proposed, including any risks and alternatives, before you decide whether you will agree to the treatment;

- to have access to your health records, and to know that those working for the NHS will, by law, keep their contents confidential;

- to choose whether or not you wish to take part in medical research or medical student training.

From 1 April 1992 there are three new rights:

- to be given detailed new information on local health services, including quality standards and maximum waiting times. You will be able to get this information from your health authority, GP or Community Health Council;

- to be guaranteed admission for virtually all treatments by a specific date no later than two years from the day when your consultant places you on a waiting list. Most patients will be admitted before this date. Currently, 90% are admitted within a year;

- to have any complaint about NHS services — whoever provides them — investigated, and to receive a full and prompt written reply from the chief executive of your health authority or general manager of your hospital. If you are still unhappy, you will be able to take the case up with the Health Service Commissioner.

There are nine standards of service which the NHS aims to provide:

- respect for privacy, dignity and religious and cultural beliefs;

- arrangements to ensure everyone, including people with special needs, can use the services;

- information to relatives and friends about the progress of your treatment, subject, of course, to your wishes;

- an emergency ambulance should arrive within 14 minutes in an urban area, or 19 minutes in a rural area;

- when attending an accident and emergency department, you will be seen immediately and your need for treatment assessed;

- when you go to an outpatient clinic, you will be given a specific appointment time and will be seen within 30 minutes of it;

- your operation should not be cancelled on the day you are due to arrive in hospital. If, exceptionally, your operation has to be postponed twice you will be admitted to hospital within one month of the second cancelled operation;

- a named qualified nurse, midwife or health visitor responsible for your nursing or midwifery care;

- a decision should be made about any continuing health or social care needs you may have, before you are discharged from hospital.

From 1 April 1992, authorities will set and publicise clear Local Charter Standards, including:

- first outpatient appointments;

- waiting times in accident and emergency departments, after initial assessment;

- waiting times for taking you home after treatment, where your doctor says you have a medical need for NHS transport;

- enabling you and your visitors to find your way around hospitals, through enquiry points and better signposting;

- ensuring that the staff you meet face to face wear name badges.

Rights of any description rest on the ethical principle of justice: everyone is — or should be — entitled to the same. The Universal Declaration of Human Rights (1948) has 30 Articles, and sets out as many rights which it declares as 'a common standard of achievement for all peoples and all nations'. If these rights and standards applied to all people everywhere, there would be no need for any further pressure groups or charters. The fact that such groups are increasingly vocal and that documents proliferate shows clearly enough that even the best-intentioned and 'universal' document cannot give a person what others prevent him or her from having.

Most of the rights which people want and need can hardly be absolute: the right to free speech, free travel, free choice of employment. Any of these rights depend on circumstances often beyond the person's control. On the other hand, the right not to be held in slavery, not to be tortured, and not to be subjected to arbitrary arrest (Articles 4, 5 and 9 of the Universal Declaration of Human Rights) should quite clearly be absolute.

Almost all the rights listed in any documents are simply basic ways of living as human beings. They are not novel rights at all, but rather dues which people have in the first place been deprived of through 'man's inhumanity to man' and now seem to be given back — with a gesture of largesse into the bargain.

What may be considered as rights by patients differ widely among individuals. Among the better-known rights sometimes cited are the rights:

- to free health care at the point of need;

- to refuse treatments;

- to confidentiality;

- to full and frank explanation of diagnosis and prognosis;

- to die peacefully;
- to be treated with dignity;
- not to be harmed.

These rights are claims which can be made against those who hold the corresponding duties. For someone to say that he or she has a right to free health care at the point of need means that someone has to provide that care. The fact that a journal called *Iatrogenics* even exists fundamentally questions who has what rights and responsibilities when it comes to diseases caused by 'the medical care process' (*Bulletin of Medical Ethics* 1991).

- Mr T Jones, a taxi driver in a large town, had a sore throat for two weeks and went to his GP. He took one look at Mr Jones' throat and sent him to the local hospital's ENT clinic. Assessment was swift, and Mr Jones was soon given a four-week course of radiotherapy. At the follow-up appointment in the clinic he saw the doctor he had originally seen. This doctor looked at notes, X-rays, the patient, and back again to the notes. Mr Jones began to be suspicious that something was wrong. Then the doctor asked if he was Mr T Jones. Yes, he was. Then Mr J Jones had not received the necessary radiotherapy . . . Mr Jones' suspicions began to take a different turn.

Dickson (1982) lists some 11 rights which people have, among them 'the right to make mistakes' (p. 32). The doctor in this case may very well have been feeling like invoking that right. However, a doctor also has a duty 'not to do harm', which is recognised as one of the specific ethical principles in medicine and the one which overrides any right or claim. Mr Jones may well invoke that right, and seek compensation. Rights, based on the principle of justice, have then to be countered by legislation which can and ought to enforce the right.

Justice, however, is not the only principle which applies

to patients' rights. The principle of truth-telling or honesty is equally important, and can be seen as the right to full and frank explanation and discussion of prognosis and diagnosis. Mr Jones may not have been too curious about his illness, and not understood too much about anatomy, disease processes or particular treatments. He may have thought that the doctor knew what he was doing and left it at that. And the doctor may have thought or assumed exactly the same, particularly given Mr Jones' job and therefore possible social class. So, not much was said between the two — and clinics being busy places the doctor may have been pleased that he did not have to spend much time explaining.

In this sense, what is *not* said is as important as what *is* said. Had some explanation been offered the patient may have realised that something may have been wrong.

The patient may in this sense not only have a right to know and to be treated. He may also have a duty to know everything necessary before he is treated. It is the case that when one principle or right is infringed, other principles and rights will also be. Thus, had honesty or truth existed, doing no harm may also have existed.

How a right is applied to others depends on how those others interpret the responsibility of the one against whom a claim is made. This is where the relationship comes into focus. Did the doctor in this case work from the idea of a code or contract, or did he consider the idea of a covenant, that is of responding to the patient as a person, and relating to him? If he applied a code, he would have been aware of having to uphold certain standards, such as giving adequate care. If he applied the idea of a contract, he would have been aware of his boundaries, and not 'got involved'. However, he would have cared about informed consent. No doubt he had told Mr Jones about radiotherapy, and Mr Jones had agreed. But had he told him about the possible side effects, the long-term damage, etc?

Most likely not. It is not simply a matter of getting through the workload, or being efficient; it is also a matter of communication, and that is always a matter of relationships: how we communicate with each other matters most particularly. The relationship, however, is based not just on measurable rights and principles, but also on human values, and on how people are human with each other.

As well as the specific story of Mr Jones, the rights which patients in the 'Victoria' ward story (above) had can also be examined in more detail.

The right mostly infringed here was that of being treated with dignity. This is necessarily a rather 'inexact' right, and one would first have to establish what is meant by 'dignity'. Complaints have often been heard from patients about the loss of dignity in clinics where changing rooms were inadequate, or at teaching rounds where patients were left naked for long periods while students prodded and gazed at some physical sign. To be shunted around the ward, left in a draughty corner close to the sluice with its noise and smells and the door not closing well, and without adequate bedding, must surely be undignified, even degrading. If one of those patients had claimed the right to be treated with dignity at that time, a nurse would have had a duty to consider her responsibility of respect for the person and do something practical to give the patient her right. What this might have entailed on the spot can only be guessed: telephone calls, discussions, statements, managers coming and going, and probably more confusion, chaos and work for the nurses. It seems trite to say that prevention is better than cure. However, when a nurse is conscious of responsibilities *vis-à-vis* patients and clients, the nurse will — or should at least endeavour to — ensure that a patient need not invoke a right. Part of a nurse's responsibility in promoting health means anticipating possible situations and not only responding to demands for care.

All the rights listed above — and those variously claimed by people at times — are based on the notions of human dignity and the corresponding responsibility of respect for the person.

Certain groups of patients have established rights for themselves. The various associations for specific types of illness, such as cancer, diabetes, multiple sclerosis, etc, not only give support and advice and foster research, but also act as pressure groups and campaign for better understanding and care of their members. The Labour Party is at present (1992) inviting comments on a draft charter for users of residential/nursing care, entitled *Happy to be Home* (Rooker 1991). CancerLink, a support group for patients with cancer, has published a *Declaration of Rights of People with Cancer* to act as a starting point for debate about how the needs of people with cancer are being met and how service provision could be improved.

Declaration of Rights of People with Cancer. Reprinted with permission of CancerLink, London

I have the right:

1. . . . to equal concern and attention whatever my gender, race, class, culture, religious belief, age, sexuality, lifestyle, or degree of able-bodiedness.

2. . . . to be considered with respect and dignity, and to have my physical, emotional, spiritual, social and psychological needs taken seriously and responded to throughout my life, whatever my prognosis.

3. . . . to know I have cancer, to be told in a sensi-

tive manner and to share in all decision-making about my treatment and care in honest and informative discussions with relevant specialists and other health professionals.

4. . . . to be informed fully about treatment options and to have explained to me the benefits, side effects and risks of any treatment.

5. . . . to be asked for my informed consent before I am entered into any clinical trial.

6. . . . to a second opinion, to refuse treatment or to use complementary therapies without prejudice to continued medical support.

7. . . . to have any special welfare needs acknowledged and benefit claims responded to promptly.

8. . . . to be employed, promoted or accepted on return to work according to my abilities and experience and not according to assumptions about my disease and its progression.

9. . . . to easy access to information about local and national services, cancer support and self help groups and practitioners that may be useful in meeting my needs.

10. . . . to receive support and information to help me understand and come to terms with my disease, and to receive similar support for my family and friends.

(This document is also available in Hindi, Urdu, Punjabi and Chinese.)

One of the difficulties about patients' rights is that it is as yet impossible to establish definite rights. 'Even those

who argue for welfare rights often fail to show who
should bear the demanding counterpart obligations'
(O'Neill 1991). This may be partly because of the tradition
of hierarchies in health care. The higher up in the hierarchy a person is, the more diffuse and less clearly defined
the responsibilities become. The model of circles outlined
in this chapter, with every worker directly responsible to
the patient, may go some way to seeing and approaching
the problem differently. Another of the difficulties with
patients' rights has to do with language.

To claim a right usually presupposes conflict. For
instance, the right to die with dignity is usually invoked
by and for patients who prefer palliative care to heroic
efforts to save their lives. Yet without adequate facilities
and training of the personnel, asserting such a right is
empty.

Rights usually also centre on an individual when clearly
the basic goods of welfare cannot be provided on an
individual basis. This is shown in the story of 'Victoria'
ward. If one patient had invoked the right to be treated
with dignity, then all the other patients may have done
the same. Yet even if a group of patients got together,
this may still only have concerned the patients on that one
ward, and patients on other wards in similar circumstances may still not have benefited. For the right of that
one patient or group of patients to be met, a vast number
of people and organisations would need to be involved,
among them the laundry delivery system, the building
maintenance system, the authority which plans new buildings and decides when they should be built, the nursing
staff duty rostering, the allocation of student nurses, and
so forth. Before equality between an individual's rights
and their fulfilment exists, at least in the welfare system,
a great many systems and structures have to work hand
in hand, each conscious of an equal measure of responsibilities and rights.

Lastly, the language of rights tends to 'emphasize negative rights, that is, the *protection* of what one has, and not positive rights, or the *provision* of what one needs' (Jameton 1984, p. 141). This would be tantamount to saying, 'I have a responsibility to see that my patients' rights are upheld and I insist on that responsibility and want it carried out'.

This is indeed what is happening in many places and in various ways, when nurses take on the mantle of patient advocate (see chapter 3 for a full discussion of this topic). A nurse advocate has to be familiar with the language and concept of rights. One such example was reported by Devine (1990). Nurses in the Lothian and Glasgow areas of Scotland were concerned:

> about cutbacks at their place of work. Staffing levels were being reduced without consultation or agreement. Overtime was cut back. Newly qualified nurses were not getting jobs. Training budgets were cut by 50% and there was a freeze on the purchase of new equipment. Yet against this background of cutbacks, patient throughput was being maintained and in some areas increased.

The nurse members of COHSE (Confederation of Health Service Employees) were encouraged to take their advocacy role seriously and write to their immediate managers, quoting Clauses 11 and 12 of the UKCC Code of Conduct and Part C of *Exercising Accountability* (UKCC 1989). The response from management 'had an immediate effect in the form of additional nurses or, in the case of community staff, a reduction in caseloads'.

The Patient's Moral Rights

Moral rights do not necessarily have legal backing, but moral rights are backed by general opinion or good reason or both (Jameton 1984, p. 139). An example of this is that only in 1991 did women in Britain gain the legal right not to be raped by their husbands, although they had the moral right all along. Jameton (1984) believes that 'sometimes when people say "we have a moral right to X", they mean, "we have a moral right to X, and there should, morally, be a legal right to X". Many people who defend a right to health care claim something of this form' (p. 139).

Several of the points made above under responsibilities could also be cited here. When one person considers responsibilities seriously, this also implies that that person acts morally, that is, brings about something good in a situation of conflict without abusing any power. Kant's Practical Imperative of 'Treat every human being, including yourself, always only as an end and never as a mere means' has often been quoted as the epitome of moral action. However, without it — or some similar statement — society would be in danger of disintegration. A moral right, in this sense, cannot be demanded; it can only be given by people who act morally.

The Nurse's Legal Rights

Many of the nurse's rights have already been mentioned above. This shows again how difficult it is to separate the subject of rights and responsibilities.

Nurses' legal rights are, firstly, those which the employing authority gives them: the right to working in a safe and healthy environment; the right to a salary paid on time; the right to holidays and sick leave. These are statutory rights, and although the circumstances of them may vary from place to place, they are the same rights for all nurses in Britain.

Secondly, the profession gives nurses the right to practise their profession within the parameters set down by the regulatory body and as long as those nurses uphold the Code of Professional Conduct.

In certain areas of work individual nurses may have additional rights, such as limited drug prescribing. Such rights will however be clearly defined and monitored.

Wherever they work, nurses also have rights — mostly unwritten — similar to those which patients claim: rights to be treated with dignity and respect; to have confidentiality maintained in matters of personal records or information shared with superiors as appropriate; not to be harmed in the course of duty.

Nurses have the right to further education and to supervision and support. Although these elements are also the nurse's personal responsibility (UKCC Code Clauses 3 and 4), they are now often perceived as rights because too frequently they are lacking. In the light of this chapter, it is questionable how far these rights can be fully claimed and received. However, in order to understand personal, moral and legal responsibility, and carry it out, these areas too, must be considered and investigated.

An interesting document has been produced by the ICN in Jamaica in 1991 regarding the violation of the human rights of nurses. This states, among other things, that because 'violations of the human rights of nursing and other health personnel are occurring in many countries where, in the course of their health related work, such persons are seen to be in conflict with the government', the ICN will investigate such incidents, will keep those involved in each case up to date, and will 'in most instances publish data on specific incidents of human rights abuses that the organisation is working on'.

This document does not establish a right for nurses, but is welcome as a statement of concern by nursing's highest organisation that it will care for its members.

The Nurse's Moral Rights

If there is one right which could be added to this list by calling it a 'moral right', it would be 'the right to be listened to and heard' by colleagues and in particular by superiors.

One of the greatest difficulties in human relationships is listening and being listened to. Assumptions are made, and people's stories are dismissed as trivial, the result often being misery and degradation. Had the doctor listened to Mr Jones and his story, and taken time to hear it, he might have heard something which might have prevented wrong treatment being given. Had the managers of the nurses on 'Victoria' ward listened to their stories about difficulties with bed allocations, with buildings, with linen supplies, etc., much grief could have been avoided.

The sad fact is that the higher up in the hierarchy people are, the less time they usually have, and the better judges they consider themselves to be of situations they only know second-hand. Yet the opposite is true for real human living and responding. If each worker is listened to, he or she knows quite adequately how to respond in the given parameter of care, but without being listened to, a person does not have the moral freedom to act. Listening is not just the answer; it is also the starting point of any ethical acting and of understanding what responsibilities and rights are about.

References

Bulletin of Medical Ethics (1991) Points, 7.

Campbell, A.V. (1984) *Moderated Love*. London, SPCK.

Chapman, C.M. (1980) The rights and responsibilities of nurses and patients. *Journal of Advanced Nursing*, **5**: 127–134.

Devine, J. (1990) Exercise your rights. *Nursing Times*, **86**(21): 30–1.

Dickson, A. (1982) *A Woman in Your Own Right*, London, Quartet Books.

Hannah, A. (1991) *Legal Responsibility*. Paper delived at National Centre for Nursing and Midwifery Ethics, Queen Charlotte College, London, on 13 April 1991.

Hunt, G. (1991) *The Concept of Moral Responsibility*. Paper delivered at National Centre for Nursing and Midwifery Ethics, Queen Charlotte College, London, on 13 April 1991.

ICN (1973) *International Council of Nurses: Code for Nurses*. Geneva, ICN.

ICN (1991) *ICN's Role in the Violation of the Human Rights of Nurses*. Geneva, ICN.

Jameton, A. (1984) *Nursing Practice, the Ethical Issues*. Englewood Cliffs, NJ, Prentice-Hall.

Lambourne, R. (1983) In *Explorations in Health and Salvation*, M. Wilson (ed.), University of Birmingham.

May, W.F. (1975) Code, covenant, contract or philanthropy. *Hastings Center Report 5*, December.

Niebuhr, H.R. (1963) *The Responsible Self*. New York, Harper & Row.

Noddings, N. (1984) *Caring. A Feminine Approach to Ethics and Moral Education*. Berkeley, CA, University of California Press.

O'Neill, O. (1991) Introducing ethics: some current positions. *Bulletin of Medical Ethics*, **73**: 18–21.

Rooker, J. (1991) *Happy to be Home*. Draft for consultation of Labour's Charter for users of residential/nursing care. London, House of Commons.

The Patient's Charter (1991) London, HMSO.

Tschudin, V. (1992) *Ethics in Nursing, the Caring Relationship* (2nd edn.). Oxford, Butterworth Heinemann.
Turner, T. (1990) Crushed by the system? *Nusing Times*, **86** (49): 19.
UKCC (1992) *Code of Professional Conduct* (3rd edn.). London, UKCC.
UKCC (1989) *Exercising Accountability*. London, UKCC.
Veatch, R. (1972) Models for ethical medicine in a revolutionary age. *Hastings Center Report 2*, June.

Further Reading

Baly, M.E. (1984) *Professional Responsibility* (2nd edn.). Chichester, John Wiley.

This is a basic text which sets out nurses' rights and responsibilities simply and clearly.

Johnstone, M-J (1989) *Bioethics, a Nursing Perspective*. Sydney, W.B. Saunders.

An exciting and comprehensive textbook. A lengthy chapter on patients' rights looks at that subject in great detail.

Tschudin, V. (1992) *Ethics in Nursing, the Caring Relationship* (2nd edn.). Oxford, Butterworth Heinemann.

Chapter 6 is concerned with rights and responsibilities in some detail.

CHAPTER 5

Accountability

Diane Marks-Maran

Accountability and responsibility go closely together, but they are not the same. One makes the other legitimate. Accountability is about justifying actions by understanding their reasons and possible consequences. There are different aspects of accountability, and they are all separately examined in this chapter, although they clearly overlap. Understanding accountability will help nurses to understand their actions and decisions, and enable them to be more creative at all levels of work.

Introduction

Recently, while travelling on the number 207 bus in West London, there was an inordinate amount of traffic and the bus had been at a standstill for a good five minutes about 200 yards from the next bus stop. A man was waiting by the exit doors for the bus to arrive at the stop and after a while began to get impatient that the bus wasn't moving due to the traffic and the stop was just up the road. He asked the driver to open the doors, to let him out there. The driver's response was 'I can't do that mate, we've been told not to open the doors except at bus stops and it's more than my job's worth'. In this situation, the driver knew his responsibilities — what action he was expected to take — and was unwilling to deviate from his expected action.

What has this to do with accountability in nursing?

It is difficult, if not artificial, to examine the notion

of accountability without also explaining the notion of responsibility (see chapter 4). Accountability and responsibility are often mistakenly used synonymously. Yet, there is a difference between the two. The term 'responsibility' may indicate actions which a nurse is to take in a given situation, eg a nurse is responsible for ensuring that a patient is correctly prepared for operation. By doing a number of tasks or procedures, nurses are able to fulfil their responsibilities. In many respects, this is little different from the driver of the 207 bus not opening the doors between bus stops.

However, the nurse is not only responsible for taking certain nursing actions, but should also be able to explain why these actions were taken, or as Burnard and Chapman (1988) state 'must understand its origins, and the powers of carrying it out'. This is what accountability is:

justifying actions by understanding the rationale behind them and the possible consequences of such actions.

An accountable person does not undertake an action merely because someone in authority says to do so. Instead, the accountable person examines a situation, explores the various options available, demonstrates a knowledgeable understanding of the possible consequences of options and makes a decision for action which can be justified from a knowledge base.

It is also worth noting that a person can be *responsible* for something and yet may not be required to *account* for it. An example of this is the student nurse or health care assistant who might be held responsible for carrying out an action but may not have the knowledge or experience to understand fully the rationale for that care, identify other options and consequences and therefore make an informed decision about the action. Instead, the student carries out the delegated responsibility while the trained nurse assumes accountability.

There is a third notion, that of authority, which also needs to be examined. In order to be accountable, a nurse requires the authority to act. In nursing, however, bureaucratic and inflexible practices and traditions have militated against nurses acting as accountable practitioners by denying authority for nursing decisions to the individual nurse in favour of insisting that only those in senior positions have authority for making nursing decisions. This has created a sub-culture of nurses who are unable or unwilling to exercise accountability in the face of the 'sister said so' syndrome. Conversely, some nurses have used the excuse of 'I have to do as I'm told' to avoid the need for making autonomous nursing decisions and therefore avoid having to account for their actions.

This chapter will examine the notions of accountability and its relationship to responsibility and authority from a number of perspectives: legal accountability, managerial accountability, professional accountability and moral accountability. In doing so, it will become obvious that as well as there being large areas of overlap between these four types of accountability, there are often instances when they are in direct conflict with each other.

Legal Accountability

If I am driving my car down a road at 60 miles per hour when there are signs saying that the road has a 40 mph speed limit, am I breaking the law?

Clearly I am. The law says that the speed limit is 40 mph. In travelling at 60 mph, I am going against the legal speed limit. But is what I am doing wrong? Again, in terms of the law I am doing wrong. However, what if I have a seriously ill child in the back of the car and I am rushing that child to hospital? Am I still breaking the law? Clearly I am. The law still says that this road has a 40 mph speed limit and I am exceeding that speed limit. But is what I am doing wrong?

Here we have a conflict between what the law says is right and what I believe to be right in this situation. As a resident of Britain I am responsible for adhering to the laws of the land and I can be called to account for my actions with regard to the law. Benjamin and Curtis (1986) point out that circumstances may excuse me for violating the law but they do not suspend the law.

In Britain voluntary active euthanasia is against the law and a nurse or doctor who deliberately takes an action with the sole intention of bringing about the death of another person will most likely be accused of, or charged with, murder. This is regardless of whether or not the nurse's or doctor's intention was benevolent. The action taken is legally wrong. However, it may not necessarily be morally wrong. If, for example, a person believes that people have a fundamental right to 'authentically exercise their freedom of self-determination' (Gadow 1983), even if that person's preferences are seen as foolish by others, then it could be argued that a nurse or doctor who takes an action deliberately to end another person's life (at that person's request) is acting in a morally right way.

Most nurses are familiar with another area of conflict between legal and moral accountability; that of following a prescription. If a patient's prescription states 20mg of a controlled drug four hourly for pain, but the patient is in severe pain after only two hours, what should the nurse do?

Morally, the nurse may feel that if the patient is in pain, the dosage is too low, and if she can get another nurse to countersign, she will give the patient another dose because caring means that the patient should not suffer. Legally, however, the nurse has overstepped the prescription and she will have to account for her actions.

In accounting for our actions with regard to the law we apply the same definitions and processes of accountability as was described earlier in this chapter. As residents or citizens of a country we are legally responsible to obey the laws of the land, and as nurses we are responsible to our profession.

In the case of my driving at 60 mph on a road with a 40 mph speed limit, if I am stopped by the police I will be called upon to justify (account for) my actions through explaining the rationale behind them. As a nurse, I have to explain my actions not only to the doctor, but also possibly to a disciplinary hearing. In law, I may have to face the legal consequences even though I am sure of the moral rightness of my actions in trying to get the seriously ill child quickly to hospital, or relieve the suffering patient's pain.

Consider this further scenario:

- A nursing assistant in a residential home for elderly people is asked to bath one of the residents. In carrying out this delegated responsibility, the nursing assistant places the elderly woman in a scalding hot bath. The woman subsequently dies from the scalds and from shock, and legal action is taken against the nursing assistant for manslaughter. In accounting for her actions, the nursing assistant gives as her defence (justification) the argument that no one (eg the trained nurses) ever taught her about how hot the temperature of bath water should be and, therefore, the nursing staff should have ensured that she was properly trained to take on the responsibility of bathing the residents. The outcome is that the nursing assistant is found to be guilty in law of causing the death of the elderly woman because knowing when a bath is too hot is 'common sense', rather than being a skill which requires specific or special training and knowledge.

This case raises some issues related to the responsibility of trained nurses to ensure that students or unqualified staff are adequately supervised or trained to carry out tasks which nursing staff delegate to them. As mentioned earlier, qualified nurses can be called to account, both managerially and professionally, for care delegated to, and carried out by, unqualified staff.

Tingle (1990) points out that 'nurses must be prepared for ambiguity and uncertainty in [this] complex area' because neither the UKCC Code of Professional Conduct (1992), nor the advisory document *Exercising Account-ability* (1989), nor the law, claims to provide all the answers. Legal accountability often remains in conflict with moral accountability.

Managerial Accountability

Managerial accountability is concerned with justifying our actions to those who employ us or who act as our managers on behalf of the employing authority. In whatever job we have as nurses, we may be called to answer for our actions to the person who is our line manager.

As employees, we are responsible for fulfilling our contractual obligations, our job descriptions and for working within the policies and procedures laid down by our employers. All these serve as the parameters by which we undertake our responsibilities. As such, we may be called upon to account for our professional decisions and actions taken in the course of our work as employees within our organisation. In the exercise of managerial accountability the accountable person examines a situation regarding responsibilities within a contract, explores various options and the possible consequences of options, and makes a decision which can be justified, from a knowledge base, to a manager. Within managerial accountability the notion of authority to act is important. The accountable person in a managerial context is very aware of lines of authority and, in particular where authority to act begins and ends. This may involve having to clarify — perhaps in writing — the details of what authority for managerial decisions the individual nurse has and where that authority ends.

The following story, recounted by Hunt (1991), clearly shows managerial accountability when it is considered in the light of resuscitation orders for children.

> A three year old child is dying of lymphosarcoma. After three months of visits to the hospital everyone feels that this will be her last admission. The child knows that she will soon die, and she has already asked her mother, in the presence of a nurse, what it is like to die. Her mother told her: "Well, you know what its like when you fall

asleep on the divan and I pick you up to take you upstairs to bed, and you don't know anything about it. Well, its something like that; only this time it will be God who picks you up and takes care of you."

The child was pleased with this and was ready to die. One night on the ward, while her mother is taking a rest elsewhere, the child awakes in great distress. She is struggling to breathe, obviously near death and looking very frightened. The nurse quickly calls for the doctor and mother, and remembering the story which the mother had told the child about death, picks her up and holds her gently. The child calms down, and dies peacefully in the arms of the nurse. A few minutes later the doctor arrives and castigates the nurse in the strongest possible terms, demanding to know why she has not attempted resuscitation. The nurse replies that she has simply done what she knew to be right. The doctor angrily responds: "who are you to make such a decision!" The following day the nurse is disciplined. This does not convince her that she acted wrongly; quite the reverse — it convinces her that something is morally wrong with the institution in which she works [which states that all children must be resuscitated].

Managerial accountability can be in conflict with both professional accountability and moral accountability. As with legal accountability, this is a complex area. Policies and procedure manuals may help, but when applied to individual cases they may cause harm rather than solve problems.

Professional Accountability

One of the interesting questions to ask is 'When can an occupational group call itself a profession?'

Traditionally, clergymen, doctors and lawyers were the only categories of 'professionals'. Now it is common for various sports figures to be called 'professionals'. Burnard and Chapman (1988) suggest that there are certain attributes of a professional group:

- Use of a body of specific knowledge based on research.
- Passage of this knowledge and skills of that preference to new entrants are directed by the profession itself.
- The needs of the client are paramount to the professional.
- Professionals tend to develop their own sub-culture.
- Accountability for standards of practice is judged by fellow professionals.

This final attribute is a useful way of explaining the concept of professional accountability.

Etzioni (1969) wrote that 'the ultimate justification of a professional act is that it is, to the best of the professional's knowledge, the right act'. This begs the question: right for whom? The UKCC Code of Professional Conduct (1992) identifies 16 guidelines for standards of professional practice. The Code is not law. It is a guideline indicating what the profession has decided constitutes appropriate conduct of its members. In the exercise of professional accountability, it is the UKCC as our statutory body who can call us to account for our professional conduct and it is these 16 guidelines in the UKCC Code that we can be called to account for.

If it is the statutory body which determines what is professionally a 'right' act, is it then also true that what is professionally 'right' is also morally 'right'? In the light of events such as the Graham Pink case in Stockport, it clearly does not follow that what is professionally right is that which is morally right. Pink made a moral decision with regard to making public his concern about the standards of care offered to elderly patients in his unit. In the exercise of managerial accountability, he was deemed not to be able to justify his actions within his contractual obligations (*Nursing Standard* 1991). Some people felt that he had not been able to justify his actions within his professional guidelines (the UKCC Code of Conduct). Clause 10 of the Code, related to breaching confidentiality, is one aspect cited in the Graham Pink case. If this clause applies Mr Pink could have been deemed to be unable to justify his actions to the satisfaction of the profession as laid down by the UKCC.

In fact, Mr Pink was found not to have breached the UKCC Code and could therefore satisfactorily account for his actions (*Nursing Times* 1991). This highlights the fact that managerial accountability and professional accountability can often be in conflict with each other. The criteria against which we exercise managerial accountability seem to be different from those against which we exercise professional accountability.

What is important to highlight, too, is that the 'rightness' of a professional act — one which can be justified (accounted for) from a knowledge base — does not guarantee that the person taking that seemingly 'right' action will not have to face painful consequences. 'Rightness' of an action in managerial terms may be different from the 'rightness' of an action in professional terms. This suggests that Etzioni's statement, cited earlier, about the justification of a professional act, may be confusing professional accountability with moral accountability.

Moral Accountability

Both the law and the Code of Professional Conduct are guided by ethical principles, but both the law and an ethical code of conduct are not absolute statements of truth about what is right. As demonstrated earlier, an action can be against the law but still be justified as a right action, with the person taking that action being able to account for breaking the law.

There may be times when what seems a 'right' action by our own personal value systems is contrary to the parameters laid down by law, the parameters laid down by our contractual obligations, and to the parameters laid down by the Code of Professional Conduct. This is the domain of moral accountability.

The process of exercising moral accountability is no different from the process of exercising any other type of accountability. An individual examines a situation, explains the various options available, demonstrates a *knowledgeable* understanding of the possible consequences and makes a decision which can be justified from that *knowledge base*.

In moral accountability, the *knowledge base* is the clarification of our own personal values: what is right or wrong for us. There can be no prescriptions, laws, codes or job descriptions for moral accountability. The criteria against which we make morally responsible decisions are our own personal value systems. However, in order to justify such a decision, we need to know and clarify our values and be 'at home' with that which is right or wrong.

Hunt (1991) said that 'morality, like your bus ticket, is non-transferable. No one can tell you what is morally right'. However, others (doctors, managers, the law) may try to persuade us, in the name of clinical science, the good of the organisation or the good of society that something is right. In moral terms an action is only right if it is right for the person taking the action, not because of moral blackmail disguised as clinical expertise or managerial practice.

Perhaps Etzioni's statement could be re-written to read: the ultimate justification of a *moral* act is that it is, to the best of the person's knowledge, the right act.

With reference to the Graham Pink case, it seems likely

that Mr Pink made a moral decision which he justified on the basis of the moral rightness of the decision. The dilemma here is that what is morally right (and morally justified) may not be judged as being managerially right (managerially justified). In exercising moral accountability, it is possible that a person cannot excuse managerial accountability.

There is little difference between this scenario and that described earlier of the person breaking the speed limit in order to get a sick child to hospital, or the nurse not resuscitating a dying child. In both these decisions, a moral decision took priority over either a managerial or legal one. The result is the same: the person can justify the action in moral terms, but not in either managerial or legal terms. Woodruff (1985) said that 'Though the relationship between the law and ethics must be acknowledged, it must also be stressed that . . . the law may not be relied upon as a substitute for individual or professional ethical examination'.

The advisory document *Exercising Accountability* (1989) states that:

> Accountability is an integral part of professional practice, since, in the course of that practice, the practitioner has to make judgements in a wide variety of circumstances and be answerable for those judgements. (p. 6)

> Each practitioner must determine exactly how this aspect of personal professional accountability is satisfied within her particular sphere of practice. This requires the exercise of judgement as to the 'when' and 'how'. The practitioner must be sure that it is the interests of the patient or client being promoted rather than the patient or client being used as a vehicle for the promotion of personal or sectional professional interests. The Code of Professional Conduct envisages the role of the patient or client advocate as an integral and essential aspect of good professional practice. (p. 12)

Conclusion

Nurses have a history of making judgements similar to the driver of the 207 bus who was cited in the introduction to this chapter. In a small, informal survey of trained nurses undertaken by me in 1978 (unpublished), forty-three nurses were asked at different times of the day why they were undertaking a particular nursing task or activity at that time. Sixty-eight per cent of the replies came into three categories of answer: (1) Sister (or Doctor) said so; (2) we've always done it this way; (3) I don't know. Clearly these nurses were unable to account for their actions in a way which demonstrated that they had examined the situation or had explored options available from a knowledgeable understanding of the consequences. As a result they could not demonstrate that they could justify their actions from a knowledge base.

This chapter has attempted to examine four dimensions of accountability and their relationships with the concepts of responsibility and authority. Clearly there are conflicts between each type of accountability. Nurses need to have a good understanding of each type of accountability, the conflicts between them, the consequences of the decisions they take about their practice, and the appropriate knowledge-base to exercise accountability, whatever form that may take.

References

Benjamin, M. and Curtis, F. (1986) *Ethics in Nursing* (2nd edn.). Oxford, Oxford University Press.

Burnard, P. and Chapman, C. (1988) *Professional and Ethical Issues in Nursing*. Chichester, John Wiley.

Etzioni, A. (1969) *The Semi-Professionals and Their Organisation*. New York, Free Press.

Gadow, S. (1983) Existential advocacy. In Murphy and Hunter (eds.) *Ethical Problems in the Nurse-Patient Relationship*, Boston, Allyn & Bacon.

Hunt, G. (1991) *Moral Responsibility in Nursing*. Paper presented at the Inaugural Conference of the National Centre for Nursing and Midwifery Ethics, Queen Charlotte's College, 13 April 1991.

Nursing Standard (1991) Pink sacked but speaks up for whistle blows. **6**(1): 6.

Nursing Times (1991) Sacked Mr Pink fights on. **87**(39): 6.

Tingle, J. (1990) Accountability and the law: how it affects the nurse. *Senior Nurse*, **10**(2): 8–10.

UKCC (1992) *Code of Professional Conduct* (3rd edn.). London, UKCC.

UKCC (1989) Exercising Accountability. London, UKCC.

Woodruff, A. (1985) Becoming a nurse: the ethical perspective. *International Journal of Nursing Studies*, **22** (9): 295–302.

Index

accountability
  and authority 123, 127
  and common sense 126
  conflict between legal and moral
    124–6
  conflict between managerial and
    moral 128
  conflict between managerial and
    professional 128, 130
  definition 122–3
  and knowledge base 131
  legal 124–6
  managerial 127–8
  moral 130–2
  phase in pattern of responsibility
    22, 26–8
  professional 128–30, 132
  reasons for actions, an informal
    survey of 133
  and responsibility 92, 94–5, 122–3
  supervision of unqualified staff
    126
advance directives (declarations) 60
advocacy 65–6
  and autonomy 65–6, 82
  bridge between the moral and the
    legal? 78
  by all professionals? 80
  by any person? 72
  case history 68
  and the concept of power 69–71
  definitions 66–8
  and ethics 78
  and excellence in caring 69, 71
  existential 73–4
  and freedom of choice 65–6, 82
  human advocacy 71–2, 73

informing and supporting the
    patient 76–8
  learned skill? 78, 81
  legalistic interpretation 75–6
  natural role? 72, 73
  within nurses' competence? 75
  nurses' unique role? 72, 80
  and relationship between nursing
    and human autonomy 79
  risks in 79
  and self-determination 74, 78
  see also nurse as advocate
American Nurses' Association
  (ANA), Code for Nurses 4
anonymity, alleged breach of 2–3
authority, and accountability 123,
  127
autonomy
  in case study 19–20
  as ethical principle 14–15
  in health care 38–9
  need for, in nurse-advocate 65–6,
    82
  and nurse's moral responsibility
    100–1
  of professional 40
  and professional–patient
    relationship 39–40
  relationship with utilitarianism 45
  in society 37–8
  value of 36–40
  see also self-determination

beneficence 11
benefit to patients
  and health care professionals 43
  QALYs as measurement of
    42–3

Benner, Patricia, on advocacy 68–71
breach of confidentiality
   by careless talk 3–4
   in case study 16, 19–20
   UKCC advice 31

cancer, rights of people with 112–13
caring
   excellence in, and advocacy 69, 71
   qualities of power 69–70
challenge, phase in pattern of
   responsibility 21, 23
co-workers, nurses' responsibilities
   to 87, 88, 89
Code for Nurses (ANA), on
   confidentiality 4
Code for Nurses (ICN)
   on confidentiality 4, 87
   on responsibilities 86–7, 91
Code of Professional Conduct for the
   Nurse, Midwife and Health
   Visitor (UKCC)
   and accountability 129
   on confidentiality 4–6, 89
   and disclosure of information 89
   on responsibilities 88–9
   and standards of professional
      practice 129
codes of practice, as upholders of
   standards 92
colleagues, nurses' responsibilities to
   87, 88, 89
common humanity, and advocacy
   71–3
communication, see informing the
   patient
complaints about NHS, patient's
   rights 106
confidentiality
   breach of, see breach of
      confidentiality
   case notes, wide availability of 3
   clash of interests? 8
   and Code of Nurses (ANA) 4
   and Code for Nurses (ICN) 4, 87
   and Code of Professional Conduct
      (UKCC) 4–6, 89

health care workers not all bound
   to 3
   and justice 13–14
   nurses' responsibilities 4, 87, 89
   patient's right to 1
   and truth 14
   see also disclosure of information
Confidentiality (UKCC Advisory
   Document) 5
   and deliberate breach of
      confidentiality 31
   and disclosure of information 5–6,
      26–7
   and trust 6–7
consent
   to disclosure of information 5,
      26–7
   for HIV testing 48
   informed, see informed consent
contracts 97
covenants 96
Curtin, Leah, on advocacy 71–3

Data Protection Act (1984) 3
Declaration of Human Rights
   (United Nations) 37–8, 108
Declaration of Rights of People with
   Cancer 112–13
deontology (Duty Ethics) 21, 85
   vs utilitarianism 8–9
dignity, being treated with 112–13
disclosure of information
   accidental 3–4, 5–6, 27
   alleged breach of anonymity 2–3
   categories of 5–6, 26–7
   creative possibilities in 28, 29
   as legal requirement 5
   with patient's consent 5, 26–7
   in the public interest 5, 6, 8–9, 27,
      29–30
   and UKCC Code of Professional
      Conduct 89
   to whom? 30–1
   see also confidentiality, breach of
Duty Ethics, see deontology

education, see training

environment of care 89, 94
ethical principles 9
  case study 16–21
  goodness or rightness 11–12
  individual freedom, see autonomy
  justice or fairness 12–14
  and the law 132
  truth-telling or honesty 14
  value of life 9–11
euthanasia, conflict between legal
    and moral accountability 124–5
Exercising Accountability (UKCC
    Advisory Document) 132

fairness, see justice
freedom of choice, see autonomy

Gadow, Sally, on advocacy 73–4
gender concept, in medicine 69,
    70–1
general practitioners, and patient's
    rights 105–6
goodness, as ethical principle 11–12
  in case study 17–18
Guide to Consent for Examination or
    Treatment (NHS) 49, 53–4

health records
  and confidentiality 3
  patient's right to access 1
helping relationship 95
HIV testing, seeking consent for 48
honesty
  case study 19, 109–11
  as ethical principle 14
human advocacy 71–2, 73
Human Rights Movement 104, see
    also Declaration of Human
    Rights
human rights of nurses, violation of
    117

ICN, see International Council of
    Nurses
individual freedom, see autonomy
information, disclosure of, see
    disclosure of information

informed consent 35–6
  advance directives (declarations)
    60
  and alternative treatments 49–54
  always to be obtained from
    patients? 57–8
  and children 61
  and disastrous outcome 61–2
  and individual autonomy 36–40
  legal implications 35, 38, 46–7
  living will 60
  moral background 36–45
  patients competent to give? 58–9
  patients incompetent to give 60–1
  patients unwilling to discuss 57–8
  and proposed treatment 45–9
  seeking 45–61
informing the patient
  duties of doctors and nurses 46–7
  effectively 54–6
  and HIV testing 48
  limits to 56–7
  role of nurse advocate 76–7
  and terminology problems 54–5
  therapeutic privilege 47, 52
  see also informed consent
institutions, rights and
    responsibilities 102–4
International Council of Nurses
    (ICN)
  and violation of human rights of
    nurses 117
  see also Code for Nurses (ICN)
interpretation, phase in pattern of
    responsibility 21–2, 22, 25–6

justice, as ethical principle 12–14
  in case study 18–19

Kohnke, Mary, on advocacy 76–9

law
  and ethics 132
  implications of informed consent
    35, 38, 46–7
  requirement to disclosure of
    information 5

see also *under* nurses'
  responsibilities; nurses' rights;
  patients' rights
life
  quality of 43
  value of, *see* value of life
listening, the need for 118
living wills 60

May, W.F., and the helping
  relationship 95–7
medical records, *see* health records
Melia, Kath, on advocacy 75–6

National Health Service (NHS)
  complaints about 106
  general standards of service 106–7
  *Guide to Consent for Examination or
    Treatment* 49, 53–4
  local standards 107
  and *Patient's Charter* 105–7
Niebuhr, H.R., and Response
  Ethics 21, *see also* pattern of
  responsibility
non-maleficence 11
nurse as advocate
  care 'for', 'of' and 'about' 79–80
  empowering the patient 70
  and individual's needs and rights
    73
  to inform and support 76–7
  and language and concept of
    rights 115
  need for autonomy 65–6, 82
  and patient's value-clarification 74
  support of patient's decision
    making 72
  see also advocacy
nurse as rescuer 77–8, 80
nurse as surrogate mother 79
nurse–patient relationship 95
  power of nurse 75
  see also professional–patient
    relationship
nurses' responsibilities
  legal 46, 91–5
  moral 100–2

personal 95–9
professional 86–9
nurses' rights
  legal 116–17
  moral 118
nursing, moral purpose of 71
nursing practice and profession
  nurses' responsibility to 87, 88–9
  training, registration and research
    91–2

paternalism
  advocacy as a form of 75
  justified 44
patients
  benefit to, *see* benefit to patients
  nurses' responsibilities to 86–7,
    88–9
  responsibilities of 96–7
  rights of, *see* patients' rights
  see also informing the patient
Patient's Charter 105–7
  and alternative treatments 49
  and confidentiality 1–2
patients' responsibilities 96–7
patients' rights
  access to health records 1
  cancer patients 112–13
  to confidentiality 1
  difficulties in establishing and
    meeting 113–14
  to be informed about treatments
    46–54
  legal 104–15
  moral 115–16
  in *Patient's Charter* 105–7
  to receive health care 12–13
  to refuse treatment 46
  in specific illnesses 112
pattern of responsibility, in
    Niebuhr's Response Ethics
    21–2
  accountability (in terms of
    relationships) 22, 26–8
  challenge 21, 23
  a cyclical pattern 29
  interpretation 21–2, 22, 25–6

response 21, 22, 23–5
social solidarity 22, 28–9
philanthropy 97
Pink, Graham 129–30, 131–2
power, masculine and feminine
    perspectives 69–70
    in case study 68, 70
prescriptions, legal *vs* moral
    accountability 125
professional–patient relationship
    and respect for autonomy 39–40
    and utilitarianism 44
    see also nurse–patient relationship
professionals
    and accountability 128–30
    attributes of 128–9
    and benefit to patients 43
    training, registration and research
        91–2
    UKCC guidelines for standards
        129
public interest, disclosure of
    information in 5, 6, 8–9, 27,
    29–30

quality adjusted life years (QALYs),
    as measurement of benefit 42–3
quality of life 43
Quinn, Carroll, on advocacy 79–81

registration of practitioners 92
relationships
    accountability in terms of 22, 26–8
    in institutions 103
    and responsibilities 97–9
    see also nurse–patient relationship;
        professional–patient
        relationship
rescuer, nurse as 77–8, 80
research, in practitioner-led
    profession 92
respect for the person 10–11, 112
    and autonomy 37
response, phase in pattern of
    responsibility 21, 22, 23–5
Response Ethics 21, *see also* pattern
    of responsibility

responsibilities
    case study, *see* 'Victoria' ward
    and *Code for Nurses* (ICN) 86–7,
        91
    and *Code of Professional Conduct*
        (UKCC) 88–9
    of institutions 102–4
    of nurses, *see* nurses'
        responsibilities
    of patients 96–7
    and rights 85
responsibility
    and accountability 92, 94–5, 122–3
    circular in concept 98–9
    for confidentiality 4
    'for' *vs* 'to' in response ethics 21
    pattern of, *see* pattern of
        responsibility
rightness, as ethical principle 11–12
    in case study 17–18
rights
    case study, *see* 'Victoria' ward
    of institutions 104
    language and concept of 115
    to be listened to 118
    to 'make mistakes' 109
    negative (protection) vs positive
        (provision) 115
    of nurses, *see* nurses' rights
    of patients, *see* patients' rights
    and responsibilities 85
    see also human rights *entries*

self-determination
    as human right 74, 78
    see also autonomy
Smith, Michael, on advocacy 79–81
social solidarity, phase in pattern of
    responsibility 22, 28–9
society
    respect for autonomy in 37–8
    utilitarianism in 42
supervision
    and accountability 126
    nurses' rights to 117
support, nurses' rights to 117

supporting the patient, in role of
nurse advocate 76–7
surrogate mother, nurse as 79

teleology 21
telling the patient, *see* informing the
patient
terminology, patients' failure to
understand 54–5
therapeutic privilege 47, 52
Thiroux, J.P., and ethical principles,
see ethical principles
training
nurses' rights to 117
as professional hallmark 91–2
treatment
alternative treatment, disclosure
of? 49–54
patients' right to information
46–54
patients' right to refuse 46
and seeking informed consent
45–9
trust 6–9
truth-telling
case study 19, 109–11
as ethical principle 14

United Kingdom Central Council
(UKCC), *see Code of
Professional Conduct*;

Confidentiality (advisory
document); *Exercising
Accountability* (advisory
document)
United Nations Universal
Declaration of Human Rights
37–8, 108
utilitarianism 21, 40–2
actions as a means to an end 41
vs deontology 8–9
in health care 42–4
and professional–patient
relationship 44
relationship with autonomy 45
in society 42

value of life, as ethical principle 9–11
in case study 16–17
life's values *vs* valuers 31–2
'Victoria' ward, case study on rights
and responsibilities 90–1
advocacy 102
institution's responsibilities 104
the need to listen 118
nurses' responsibilities 93–4, 99,
104
patients' rights 111–12, 114
theory *vs* practice 93
treated with dignity 112–13
vocabulary, patients' failure to
understand 54–5